DEDIC

This book is dedicated to a man that I have not known very long but on the other hand feel as if I have known him all my life. Pastor Jeffrey W. Arnold (Uncle "Arnie") is a man of God I never thought I would meet. Because of his great reputation in ministry and living about 1500 miles away from me in Texas, my chances of meeting up with him were just about zero.

Of course I had heard of this dynamic man of God who was a little on the "kooky" side and I really wasn't sure even if I were to befriend him if we would be able to click. When I received a phone call from him inviting me to speak at his church in Gainesville, Florida I really wasn't sure what to expect.

When I got there what happened next was totally mind-boggling. When we spent time together after each service talking about the things of the Lord, he humbled himself completely and as a new convert would had questions and questions about the Gifts of the Spirit. It was as if we had changed roles, I being the mentor and he being the student. Of course, his reputation had preceded him and I had all kinds of questions I myself wanted to ask but never had the opportunity to do so. He was like a kid in a candy store with enough money to buy whatever he wanted. I did the best I could to explain whatever I knew and he was genuinely happy that I was willing to share what I had learned on the subject.

There is something else I would like to mention as a result of our visit. For all the things that have been said about him, both good and bad, I saw a man that was completely in love with God's word. Everywhere he goes he carries around a humongous briefcase filled with tons of books. Every time we would meet at a restaurant to eat, he would go there earlier and my wife and I would find him reading and studying God's word.

It had such a profound effect on me along with the CDs and videos he gave as a token of his appreciation. I realize that after this visit God had deposited in me a greater hunger for His word. I think anybody that will read this new book will find it a little more scriptural than my previous books.

Thank you Lord for bringing this wild and crazy (but godly man) into my life.

NOT AFRAID OF THE DEEP

FINDING GOD'S TREASURE IN SECRET PLACES

GEORGE PANTAGES

George Pantages Ministries

George Pantages Ministries

Cell 512 785-6324
geopanjr@yahoo.com
Georgepantages.com

TABLE OF CONTENTS

APPRECIATION

I would like to take the time to appreciate the following people for their contribution on the publication of this book:

Michelle Levigne - Editor

Luis Villegas – Book Cover Design

Maria Pantages – Typesetting

Your professionalism and expertise rang true throughout the entire process, making my writing a whole lot better than it really is.

INTRODUCTION

When the Lord first gave me the title of this book, I knew from the get go it would be my greatest challenge. It would be the first book out of 5 that I would have to write without the use of messages I preached in the past. My first four books came to life from the notes I used in various sermons I had previously preached. This time around, God gave me the prospective titles without any leading as to what the chapters would entail. Little did I know that writing a book shortly after suffering a stroke would be so complicated. It was only then that I fully understood the complexity of the effects the stroke had on my thought processes. In the beginning I was so frustrated by the stopping and restarting that I came very close to shutting down the project entirely. I fought the negativity like I have never had to before and consequently when coming so close to calling it quits, the Lord granted me enough grace to finish that thought and continue writing. As I look back now on what the Lord has given me to write, the three chapters on presumption were revelations given on the spot. I had no clue as to what this concept was all about until God unfolded it right before my eyes. That being said I would encourage the reader to absorb these thoughts with an open mind. They might not be completely clear yet I am counting on God to finish this revelation to those that are seeking Him with an open heart and mind. Let Samuel's prayer unto God become our mantra:

… *"Speak, for Your servant hears."*

(1 Samuel 3:10)

CHAPTER 1

DEEP CALLS UNTO DEEP

Deep calls unto deep...

(Psalm 42:7)

He reveals deep and secret things; He knows what is in the darkness, and light dwells with Him.

(Daniel 2:22)

The pattern for procreation was set from the foundation of the world. To increase in number, both man and animal had to procreate kind after its kind. The process was successful only when male and female of the same species were brought together. If there was ever a case for heterosexual marriage, it is found here. But that is another story perhaps for another book. The pattern for reproduction was set in concrete, nevertheless it was not limited to the physical world.

A Spiritual Pattern for Reproduction

The spiritual world also has a pattern for reproduction and for it to work effectively both God and man must be on the same wavelength. That being said, it is only possible when God calls us to the deep.

"Can you search out the deep things of God? Can you find out the limits of the Almighty?"

(Job 11:7)

One of God's greatest priorities was to uncover deep things out of darkness.

He uncovers deep things out of darkness, and brings the shadow of death to light.

(Job 12:22)

It was never His intention to keep His creation in the dark. Shedding light was an ongoing priority in the mind of God, one that would bring blessing to His children.

If the Angel of darkness, Satan was to be exposed, it would have to happen in the light. Everything about him is magnified in the shadows. He appears bigger, stronger, wiser, more experienced, and fearless in the dark. The light exposes him to reality, and in the real world he is a dog that has a bark bigger than his bite. He cannot back up his threats because he has no authority to do so. Why then is he so successful against us? We give him permission to do so, and thus forfeiting our authority to a lesser power. We really don't have to give up our authority if we will just stick to the promises God has left us to help us through our adversity. The psalmist David left us a message to give warning to our enemy what exactly he is up against. We need to take David's words to heart.

The Lord is my light and my salvation; whom shall I fear? The Lord is the strength of my life; of whom shall I be afraid?

(Psalm 27:1)

Samuel's Call to the Deep

When the Lord decided to call Samuel to a deeper walk with Him, responding to that call was easier said than done. Samuel was just a child, and as most children would, he had difficulty discerning the voice of God. His inexperience in spiritual matters was to the point that when God began to reveal Himself and His will, he mistook the voice of God for that of Eli. It was a classic case of presumption at its finest. It did not even dawn on him that the voice could be God's. Why? Because he didn't understand that God could audibly speak to man. Furthermore, why would God take the time to speak to a young, inexperienced novice when there were more capable men to receive such important orders from Him? After a couple of false alarms as Samuel made himself available to Eli, the man of God realized that the Lord was attempting to communicate with the young lad. His instructions to Samuel were simple:

Then Eli perceived that the Lord had called the boy. Therefore Eli said to Samuel, "Go, lie down; and it shall be, if He calls you, that you must say, 'Speak, Lord, for your servant hears.'" So Samuel went and lay down in his place.

(1 Samuel 3:8-9)

The message delivered to Samuel was so far above his pay grade that it not only startled him but grieved him as well. The Lord had judged his master and the judgment would be harsh. Any time I have received a negative message from God (thank God, not many) for someone else, it has always grieved my spirit. There have been moments, in trying to back away from my responsibility that my sleep has been taken away. Nevertheless, the message had to be delivered and I just left the aftermath in the hands of God.

Unlocking the Door

Unlocking the door to the deep (i.e., supernatural), like anything else, comes in stages. The lowest level begins at the hearing stage. By definition, hearing is to be aware of sound through the ear.[1] Our awareness in many situations prompts curiosity. What does this mean? The lack of clarity limits the understanding to a lot of "hit and miss" ministry. The messages received at this level are very general and can be interpreted in many ways. The "hit and miss" factor is so intimidating that most will not venture out into the deep. Being ridiculed and laughed at is not acceptable, therefore any attempt to go deeper in God is stopped in its tracks.

The second stage involves listening. Listening requires a hearing and understanding of what someone has said and that it is important or true.[2] When Samuel's hearing turned to listening, it brought forth the understanding of his assignment. Understanding brought fear, for the message received would only bring heartbreak to Eli. Undelivered messages cause frustration, which lead to uneasiness, tension, and turmoil. Holding back excessively will cause spiritual constipation, literally making the body sick. The

12

apprehension was relieved only when Samuel delivered the bad news to his master.

The final stage, the least visited stage, is the knowing stage. Knowing shows that you have a special knowledge.[3]

> *...but the people who know their God shall be strong, and carry out great exploits.*
>
> (Daniel 11:32)

Daniel knew what he was talking about. His exploits were not only great, they were mind-boggling as well. Take a glimpse at what Daniel was able to accomplish as God released His glory upon his life:

1) By rejecting the king's rich foods, he was able to become healthier, limiting his diet to pulse.
2) He did not fear defying the king's order to pray to his God. As a result, he was thrown into the lion's den, only to come out of that ordeal completely untouched.
3) Daniel was able to interpret the king's dream without even knowing what the dream was all about.

If these are not examples of great exploits then the moon is made of cheese.

When you are able to go deeper in spiritual matters there are characteristics that are unique to your experience. One of the most important characteristics, if not the most important, is when venturing out into the deep, your character has the opportunity to be molded into the image of Christ. The footing is unsure because the muck and the mire are the major culprits causing you to slip. That being said, slipping and falling down are commonplace in the deep. Because the falling causes a lack of concentration, important messages from heaven are missed. The instructions from God's throne room are sketchy and unclear at best, making the ability to carry out our assignment that much more difficult. Unsure footing yields to uncertainty. Every move and thought is second-guessed and second-guessing yields to hesitation, which leads to double-mindedness.

> *But let him ask in faith, with no doubting, for he who doubts is like a wave of the sea driven and tossed by the wind. For let not that man suppose that he will receive anything from the Lord; he is a double-minded man, unstable in all his ways.*
>
> (James 1:6-8)

Wind-tossed waves have no control over their destiny. Whichever way the wind is blowing will determine the direction those waves will move. Unlike the Spirit-filled child of God, who knows the direction he is headed in, but also is confident in knowing as the Master is given complete control, he will get to his final destination as promised.

Christ's care for us is so far-reaching that His main objective in leading our lives is to keep us from stumbling.

> *Now to Him who is able to keep you from stumbling, and to present you faultless before the presence of His glory with exceeding joy.*
>
> (Jude 24)

If that doesn't inspire you to do great things for God, nothing will. Imagine the determination our Lord has to keep us on the up and up. He will go to the ends of the earth, spending whatever time necessary to keep us from stumbling. He is so gung ho in His desire to see us succeed, He will keep on working in our behalf until it's time to present ourselves to God in glory. It is His ultimate desire on judgment day to be able to look at a bride spotless and without wrinkle, knowing His never-ending work here on earth has paid great dividends in heaven. The best part of His efforts will be rewarded on judgment day while He ushers us into the glory of heaven with exceeding joy.

The deeper one goes into the presence of God, the more he will be encouraged to defer to his weaknesses. In a godless world controlled by Satan himself, letting our weaknesses control us in our everyday environment is foolish. Look what the apostle Paul took time to write to those who were serious about serving God wholeheartedly.

> *Therefore I take pleasure in infirmities, in reproaches, in needs, in persecutions, in distresses, for Christ's sake. For when I am weak, then I am strong.*
> (2 Corinthians 12:10)

It wasn't so much that the apostle was a sadist, trying to self-inflict misery and pain upon his life. On the other hand, his wisdom came in knowing that as the adversities began to mount up in his life, his God was able not only to take over the situation, but could also bring the desired result as everything was placed in God's hands. In God's dictionary, weak can mean strong! Suffering for Christ's sake was the understood way God used to build

His kingdom and His followers were willing to endure, so they too could follow the example set by the Master.

A Pain Worth Suffering For

In June of last year (2013), while we were ministering in California, I suffered a painful accident while jogging. In the past I had fallen down maybe about twice in twenty-five years of exercise. This time would be different. The immediate pain in my right knee could not be shaken off. I walked with a limp and every step was excruciating. The swelling was so great it looked like my right knee was going to explode. It literally grew to the size of a softball. No one was around to come to my rescue and I was forced to limp back to the car, almost crying. I had never suffered an injury so severe and painful that I came very close to canceling the rest of the three-day revival I had started the night before. As time went on, spending the rest of the afternoon attempting to lessen the pain, it only got worse. I had never canceled a meeting before, but in the back of my mind I kept on telling myself there was always a first time. The Lord began to deal with me but instead of the healing I was expecting, He not only encouraged me to go to the meeting but He decided the healing would have to wait for a later time. I landed up hobbling with throbbing pain, making my way to the church. It did not take long for me to understand why God was so adamant that I keep my appointment. When it came time for healing, there was a young lady visiting for the first time who had come to the sanctuary with the use of a wheelchair. Something in my spirit said that tonight would be her night. Any and every movement behind the pulpit caused such great pain that it was very difficult to concentrate on the message. That being said, it had given

16

God an opportunity to completely take over what I had to say. With a special anointing that fell over me, I was able to complete my assignment, and as the service progressed we got to the point where we would be ministering onto the sick. I decided to leave the young lady in the wheelchair for last, hoping that as the service progressed the faith level would increase to produce a miracle. When I finally got to her, I asked her what she was suffering from and she responded with an illness I had never heard of.

"I have transverse myelitis," she blurted out.

I found out later that it was an inflammatory process of the spinal cord. The inflammation caused weakness and numbness of the limbs as well as motor, sensory, and sphincter deficits. In some cases there is almost total paralysis and sensory loss occurred below the level of the lesion.[4] But her body had deteriorated to the point that walking without the use of the wheelchair was impossible. The pain in her lower extremities only added to the problem.

When I asked her what she wanted God to do for her that evening, she responded, "Please ask Him to take away the pain."

I prayed as she requested and God immediately relieved her of any pain in her body. Her emotions began to get the best of her as the tears began to fall. The Lord nudged me, so I went a little bit further and asked her this. "Wouldn't you like God to heal you so you could walk?"

With an astonished look on her face, she wasn't sure how to respond. Never in her wildest imagination did she think that would be possible. With her permission, I prayed again. I had the ushers stand her up and immediately she broke down in tears. She had not stood up, carrying her own weight for years, and this act of God had never come into her thought processes at all. She was so overwhelmed by God touching her body, she felt it was enough for one night. I allowed her to sit down and for the rest of the service the look of bewilderment coupled with uncontrolled tears expressed her gratitude.

For all that I had to endure physically, I remember walking out of the service that night so overwhelmed by my God it was just unexplainable. My dependence on God that evening was evident and no one could deny His power and grace, especially looking at my physical helplessness. God truly took over the situation and created an incredible miracle.

God Will Not Beg

The call to a deeper walk with God is somewhat strange in that He will not beg anyone for an audience with the King.

> *Then He said, "Go out, and stand on the mountain before the Lord." And behold, the Lord passed by, and a great and strong wind tore into the mountains and broke the rocks in pieces before the Lord, but the Lord was not in the wind; and after the wind an earthquake, but the Lord was not in the earthquake; and after the earthquake a fire, but the Lord was not in the fire; and after the fire a still small voice.*
>
> (1 Kings 19:11-12)

Demonstrative moves of God will catch the attention of anyone, whether a saint or sinner. The demonstration does not necessarily guarantee a closer walk with God. In fact, people responding to a miraculous move of the

Lord find that response to be only temporary. The hoopla created by all the noise subsides when the noise itself dies down. I remember a statement my first pastor made, which at the time I did not understand. He declared that true revival in the church does not guarantee an actual growth in numbers. In actuality, he said that revival always brings a sifting to the church. There will be some who draw closer to God and their walk grows deeper. On the other hand, once the noise calms down, those dependent on God moving in that manner are disappointed when they realize this was nothing more than a spiritual fix. In the past, I have seen many leave their walk with the Lord at the same time others have been mildly encouraged to step up their faithfulness, with the main goal of knowing God in a more personal way. If demonstration of God's Spirit was a guarantee of a closer walk with Him, our churches would be packed out with no room to spare. On the contrary, in these last days, finding faithful people and churches packed to the gills is getting more and more difficult by the day.

No Bells and Whistles Here

When God means business, He will not resort to bells and whistles. He will use a method that only those sensitive to His Spirit can respond to: a still, small voice. That voice is not necessarily an audible one, yet it is recognizable enough to know that the King of glory is speaking to us. A strange thing has happened to me since the suffering of my stroke last year (2013). I have the ability to overhear conversations all around me, while at the same time it is difficult to hear exactly what others are saying at the same table I am sitting at. Sometimes after conversations are over I will ask my wife if the person we have been conversing with was speaking in low tones because I had an extremely difficult time figuring out what they were saying. More times than not her response has been everything was normal, and that I just needed to make a better effort to pay attention to the conversation. I know there are times that I can zone out other people (a hidden talent of mine) when I choose to, but in this case I have no control over what is being said all across the room. It's like my hearing has become bionic and there are all kinds of conversations that I don't need to hear. I am aware that dogs, and perhaps other animals as well, have the ability to hear sounds at a different pitch that we as humans cannot. Another ability that we as humans find foreign to us is an animal's ability to sense ahead of time when an earthquake will strike.

These traits unique to animals are very similar to the sensitive ear of a child of God. There have been occasions when uneasiness has fallen upon me and it has nothing to do with what is going on in front of me or around me. This uneasiness cannot easily be shunned, and I have learned over many years to immediately stop what I have been doing and find a place to pray. There have been times after this incident that my children will come to me asking for forgiveness, and at the same time thanking me for being a man of prayer. They will recount to me adverse situations that were nipped in the bud simply because the Spirit of the Lord came over them and warned them to escape while it was still possible. When I have asked them more or less the time of day these occurrences happened, I am blown away to find out more times than not it was the same time my uneasiness sent me to my knees. I did not know at the time specifically what was going on, yet I knew enough about the danger they would find themselves in if I did not intercede in their behalf.

> *But God has revealed them to us through His Spirit. For the Spirit searches all things, yes, the deep things of God.*
> (1 Corinthians 2:10)

Any time anyone tells me there is no virtue in spending time alone in the presence of God, I realize they never really have gone deep enough to enjoy the benefits. Look at what God is willing to give us if we allow ourselves to get sucked into the deep things God has prepared for His children.

> *I will give you the treasures of darkness and hidden riches of secret places, that you may know that I, the Lord, who call you by your name, am the God of Israel.*
> (Isaiah 45:3)

God's Incessant Desire

The Lord has an incessant desire to reveal deep and secret things to us. We needn't feel foolish to ask of Him something that He is dying to share with anyone who will go a little bit deeper with Him into the things of God. The darkness of the deep is not a secret to Him, and He is willing to share those unseen truths that unlock the door to His storehouse. The word constantly reminds us of hidden treasure that is available for those who venture out into the deep. The deep things of God are calling us to a deeper relationship with Him; all the while His call is falling on deaf ears.

> *...that their hearts may be encouraged, being knit together in love, and attaining to all riches of the full assurance of understanding, to the knowledge of the mystery of God, both of the Father and of Christ, in whom are hidden all the treasures of wisdom and knowledge.*
>
> (Colossians 2:2-3)

There is treasure to be had in the kingdom of God, bountiful and limitless if we would just be willing to go just a little bit deeper. Don't you believe it's about time to go a step further and deeper in your understanding of spiritual things? Are you not yet tired of a "hit and miss" prayer life? There is a call to you from the deep, my friend. It is a call that will change your life forever more. God is calling. Won't you come deeper?

CHAPTER 2

NOT AFRAID OF THE DEEP

He uncovers deep things out of darkness, and brings the shadow of death to light.

(Job 12:22)

There is a connection between the deep and the dark; they go hand-in-hand. The deeper one goes into the dark, the darker it gets. Whether it is the ocean, outer space, or a cave, deep and dark spend a lot of time together. You can go from the familiar everyday routine to the unfamiliar forks in the road that seems to wind endlessly. That being said, the unfamiliar always brings along with it a good amount of fear.

I sink in deep mire, where there is no standing; I have come into deep waters, where the floods overflow me.

(Psalm 69:2)

There is no sure footing and crying only makes things worse. When our greatest sense, our eyesight, is taken away we are rendered helpless, and we not only lose our way but our confidence as well. In the physical realm we depend on our eyesight way too much and the other senses God has given to us are never fully developed. More times than not they will atrophy right before us, and never become the weapons God originally armed us with to not only be successful in Him, but to be blessed as well. Eyesight in the spiritual realm is overrated because there are situations we will be put in where our eyes will deceive us, and therefore at times in spiritual matters they do not help us one iota. There is a particular reason why God will steer us to the outer darkness and that is to uncover deep things that cannot be seen by the naked eye. I have written the next statement in prior books, but it bears repeating. **God Does Not Hide Blessings from Us but Rather for Us.** We must be willing to be led to places most others will not go, overcoming obstacles as we go deeper and deeper in the spirit world. What lurks in the shadows is only a mirage put there to scare us. It is projected bigger than what it really is to paralyze us and to keep us from the blessed destiny that God has in store for us His children. Once the obstacle is unmasked in the light it is exposed as a weak fraud, no match for our God. The spiritual benefits begin with the revelations God will unfold, and help us become more effective in the kingdom of God. God is selective in whom He will call to follow Him to deeper spiritual understanding. The Lord will not waste His time on those who have a personal agenda and in their eyes don't need God's help to figure things out. God will use mysteries and/or parables to weed out those not completely sold out to the Master's plan.

And the disciples came and said to Him, "Why do you speak to them in parables?" He answered and said to them, "Because it has been given to you to know the mysteries of the kingdom of heaven, but to them it has not been given. For whoever has, to him more will be given, and he will have abundance; but whoever does not have, even what he has will be taken away from him. Therefore I speak to them in parables, because seeing they do not see, and hearing they do not hear, nor do they understand.

(Matthew 13:10-13)

Once the riffraff were weeded out, the Lord could continue mapping out His strategies for the salvation of this world. With this method of recruitment He could focus on the most important matters at hand, training and guiding His disciples to carry on with His heartbeat, that being the saving of a lost world.

There is another reason why God steers us to outer darkness, and it has nothing to do with keeping His children under His thumb. We are steered in that direction so that we might be able to uncover deep things out of the unseen. It is paramount that we must be willing to be led to places most others will not be willing to go. Obstacles that need overcoming as we go deeper in Him are frequently there to challenge us, and are to be considered commonplace. What lurks in the shadows, then, is only a mirage put there to frighten us. These mirages will be projected bigger than what they really are to paralyze us from utilizing the spiritual weapons God has armed us with. Once the obstacles are unmasked in the light, they are exposed as a weak fraud, in reality no match for our Savior. What exactly are the spiritual benefits when all of this is put into play? At this juncture the Lord has the opportunity to allow His revelation to unfold and we become more effective in His kingdom. We leave the novice level behind, graduating to a place where the signs and wonders promised to us in His word become commonplace, producing dynamic results. At this time the Lord has the opportunity to unmask the various obstacles we have stumbled over, to be revealed in the light.

The Woman at the Well

We find a fascinating story in the book of John in chapter 4 about a woman coming to draw water at Jacob's Well. It was about 4 o'clock in the afternoon, that we find Jesus starting a conversation with this Samaritan. She is startled by the fact that He, being a Jew, would strike up a conversation not only with a woman, but a Samaritan woman at that. In those times it was considered improper for any man, especially a Jewish man, to speak in public to a strange woman (John 4:27). It certainly surprised her when He asked her for a drink of water.

> *Then the woman of Samaria said to Him, "How is it that You, being a Jew, ask a drink from me, a Samaritan woman?" For Jews have no dealings with Samaritans.*
>
> (John 4:9)

His response to her threw her completely off guard. Watch how the Lord wove His way to whet her appetite about spiritual matters.

> *Jesus answered and said to her, "If you knew the gift of God, and who it is who says to you, 'Give Me a drink,'*

you would have asked Him, and He would have given you living water."

(John 4:10)

That statement hit her right between the eyes. If she was not completely blown away by the initial conversation, then His last statement had to do it. As she mulled in her mind where in the world the Lord was going with this, these things were what she would have to consider. These were the obstacles that would ultimately challenge her faith.

1. Jews never had any dealings with Samaritans, so why then was this conversation even begun?
2. Rabbis never addressed women in public
3. Why was Jesus willing to break these laws just to speak to her?

There was only one thing going through the mind of Jesus and He was willing to take her to a deeper spiritual understanding. This was only possible when He was able to perk up her curiosity. He was determined to unmask the salvation plan by removing the darkness from her life. Immediately her defense mechanisms kicked in and she blurted out a pessimistic objection.

The woman said to Him, "Sir, You have nothing to draw with, and the well is deep. Where then do You get that living water? Are You greater than our father Jacob, who gave us the well, and drank from it himself, as well as his sons and his livestock?"

(John 4:11-12)

Her lack of understanding would not deter the Master. He then changed the conversation to a level of understanding that would not be misinterpreted. It is amazing how versatile the ministry of Jesus was, in that He had an innate ability to come to the level of comprehension of those He was ministering to. He wisely unveiled her past failures in marriage and how that the man she was living with right now, in actuality, was not her husband. With that revelation staring her in the face, all of a sudden the light finally turned on. She had been entirely blown away by this man of God and immediately left Him to go back and tell others that she had found the Messiah.

The Lord's resources will always go beyond our comprehension. The psalmist David put it this way as he wrote in the Psalm 92:

Lord, how great are Your works! Your thoughts are very deep. A senseless man does not know, nor does a fool understand this.

(Psalm 92:5-6)

Oh Lord, don't let me become senseless or a fool. Take me deeper into Your wisdom and understanding and I will know You as You really are.

Our Greatest Fear: Presumption

By definition, presumption is nothing more than overstepping our boundaries or authority, things that are done without permission or good reason.[5]

'But the person who does anything presumptuously, whether he is native-born or a stranger, that one brings

reproach on the Lord, and he shall be cut off from among his people.

(Numbers 15:30)

There will be situations in our life where inexperience and/or lack of preparation will cause a less than desired result, but on the other hand never let our efforts be considered presumptuous. Shooting from the hip, a maverick mindset, rash decisions, selfishness, and egotistical dealings misusing our gifts are examples of the weapons used by presumptuous people. The labels aforementioned always follow them and are a sign of spiritual immaturity.

Presumption Must Be Replaced by Faith

To be used mightily of God in the miraculous, you've got to be willing to replace Old Testament presumption with New Testament faith. Presumption has always had a bad rap, but for the wrong reasons. Leaders of past generations went beyond their authority by scaring anyone who tried walking by faith, assuming that walk was in reality presumption. The statement, "You better know what you're doing," put such a damper on saints of God willing to step out by faith, that the end result was a generation of Christians who would not move for God unless there was 100 percent assurance that God was going to come through with the desired result. That, my friend, is not faith.

On the other hand, there are other Christians who are moved by their emotions, or supposedly great ideas, trying to use logic, convincing themselves that what they would like to accomplish in God is a good thing. A good work is only a good work when God has commanded us to do so, anything less is nothing more than presumption. The end result is disastrous in that God has no obligation to help us because He was not in it from the beginning anyway. That being said, when we fail miserably in our efforts to please God, the misunderstanding, hurt, and confusion make our future efforts to step out by faith almost nil.

Peter's Training

It was the ultimate desire of Jesus to share with His disciples the deep things of God. Of course, this would only be possible by taking the time to train them. From the get-go, Jesus continuously encouraged them to go deeper into the things of God. In Luke chapter 5, we find an example of one of those training sessions.

> *When He (Jesus) had stopped speaking, He said to Simon, "Launch out into the deep and let down your nets for a catch."*
>
> (Luke 5:4)

The instructions to Peter from the lips of Jesus were preposterous in his mind on several levels. The command to launch out into the deep and let down their nets was something that he had been doing now for some time without any success. Wasted time and effort was all he could glean from the Master's command, understanding that Jesus knew nothing about fishing. I can picture Peter turning his back on Jesus, preparing to launch out as he was commanded and at the same time rolling his eyes in disbelief. But there was something in the voice of Jesus that convinced Peter to take a chance. Without saying another word, as Peter was completing the command, the abundance of fish caught was mind-boggling. The Scripture does not say this, but I can just picture Peter with an amazed expression on his face that said, "How did you do that?" Of course, without uttering a word the smile of Jesus said it all: It's just what I do.

The training was to continue with Peter, and of course that meant going deeper into the things of God. In Matthew 14:23-27, we find another situation where Peter's faith is put to the test. As they launched their boat from the shore, for whatever reasons Jesus was not on the boat. While their boat was reaching the deepest part of the sea, during the darkest part of the night, a storm began to rise. What was happening at that moment was nothing unusual, as fishermen they had weathered many a storm in the past. At the height of the storm, in looking out of the boat, they saw Jesus approaching them, walking on the water. It is at this point that Peter had an opportunity to shine.

And Peter answered Him and said, "Lord, if it is You, command me to come to You on the water."
(Matthew 14:28)

He had remembered his first experience in the deep and his faith had risen to allow him the courage to step out of the boat. When he took his eyes off of Jesus, he began to sink, and the Lord had to rescue him out of the deep waters. Lesson learned: when venturing off into the deep, keep your eyes always on Jesus!

Peter Takes the Love Exam

Peter's final training exercise was to see himself the way he really was. He never really saw himself as a presumptuous person, yet presumption was always at the forefront of his mistakes.

Jesus said to him, "Assuredly, I say to you that this night, before the rooster crows, you will deny Me three times."

(Matthew 26:34)

Peter immediately went into a tizzy and guaranteed Jesus that His words would not come to pass. He was so adamant that the rest of the disciples joined in, and in their words were willing to follow Jesus to the death. When the outcome unfolded the way Jesus had foretold, as a result Peter wept bitterly. Seeing yourself the way you really are can at times be devastating, and in Peter's case it left him feeling worthless.

He was still feeling the aftereffects of his failure when Jesus was crucified, so much so that after the drama of the crucifixion was over, he went back to fishing. He had been utterly crushed by his lack of fortitude in what mattered most in his life. When it really counted, his words meant nothing and it was difficult accepting the truth. When Jesus came calling him again, he was thrown for a loop. Jesus then asked Peter the same question three different times. The true meaning of Peter's response is lost in the English translation, because truthfully the Greek language in this instance uses two different words for love, *phileo* and *agape*. The word love is repeated three times in the conversation, yet the last time Jesus asked the question the word love was translated *(phileo* not *agape)* meaning do you even love me as a friend? Even if the answer from Peter was to be a yes, it would be good enough to be accepted by God. The decision was then placed in Peter's hands. If revelation was to be a normal part of his ministry, he would have to continue making an effort to find his way out into the deep, trusting God every step of the way.

The day of Pentecost would turn out to be a coming out party of sorts in Peter's ministry. As the 120 worshipers received the baptism of the Holy Ghost for the first time, it caused a ruckus in the entire city. As confusion continued to grow among the onlookers, someone had to come to the forefront and explain exactly what was going on. This responsibility eventually fell on Peter's shoulders. That is when he, along with the other disciples, stood up and he preached his famous Acts 2:38 message. The message was dynamic and the results were even more so in that 3,000 were not only baptized in water in Jesus' name, they also received the baptism of the Holy Ghost for the first time, speaking in tongues.

The Church Is Afraid of the Deep

The church body as a whole is afraid of the deep, hiding behind the guise of presumption. The young people coming up in the ranks of Pentecost are being forbidden by the older generation from launching out into the deep through their intimidation tactics. These young Christians trying to spread their wings are discouraged in doing so, and all they ever hear ringing in their ears is, "You better make sure that you know what you're doing and it is from God." "It's too risky and it will be difficult to keep your bearings." "You're just going to go off the deep end and eventually crash and become an embarrassment to everyone." Faith is not all about being sure the assignment given to you will be a success. Faith is all about hearing the voice of God, and no matter what the circumstances may be, being obedient to that voice.

I have befriended a man of God whose reputation for being a great preacher precedes him. His name is

Jeffrey W. Arnold, who pastors the United Pentecostal Church in Gainesville, Florida. No matter where he goes around the world, the Spirit of God goes with him, and dynamically so. The revelation in his messages is simple yet profound. He is highly criticized by many for his unique style of presentation because it is not the so-called "proper" way a man of God should preach. I believe, and I could be wrong, that God has allowed all of this adversity so that when his greatest challenge was to unfold, he would be ready for the fight. The Lord has pricked his heart to leave the status quo and go deeper in God to bring a better understanding of the gifts of the Spirit to the Church. Because of this newfound hunger that at times has kept him up at night, he decided to pick my brain to see if the secrets unfolding slowly about the Gifts could unfold more rapidly in his life. He invited me to speak at his church in Florida, and as we discussed that subject, I was utterly floored by his humility. If anyone else were to have seen us conversing, you would've thought that I was the mentor and he was the student. He humbled himself to glean anything he could to bring more clarity on this subject and consequently throw caution to the wind. If he was going to fail, it would be failure by commission and not by omission. Many of his compatriots have warned him not to venture out into this highly unstable area. Others, they say, have done so in the past unsuccessfully and consequently have actually run their ministries into the ground.

An Unexpected Response

I remember the excitement he showed when he was recounting a testimony of miraculous healing. He had gone overseas to minister in a conference, and when it came time for the altar call there were four deaf people who had come to the altar, seeking their healing. Long story short, after he prayed the Lord miraculously unstopped their ears and they could hear perfectly. When he got back to the States, he immediately began to tell some friends of the results he had in England. One friend amongst the many immediately changed the subject on him, talking about a golf game of sorts. Initially, Pastor Arnold thought he had miscommunicated the message. After repeating it again and receiving the same results, he was taken aback by the comments. What came next was even more bewildering. That man adamantly advised him not to get involved in that "junk." Too many good men in the past had gone out into the deep and drowned, losing everything they had accumulated. Their lives, ministries, their marriages, and families as well were thrown to the wayside because of their unwise decisions. Needless to say, Pastor Arnold ended the conversation somewhat dismayed.

At a Crossroad

Being at the crossroads once again in his ministry, a decision had to be made. Will I keep it plain and simple, playing it safe, or will I be willing to launch out to deeper waters? The decision to move on to a deeper relationship with God has cost him, and will continue to do so as he goes deeper and deeper. But this is the type of man God is looking for in this last hour, one who is not afraid of the deep.

He uncovers deep things out of darkness, and brings the shadow of death to light.

(Job 12:22)

It was in God's plan from the very beginning to uncover deep things out of the darkness. If that be true, and we know that it is, then why are we so afraid of the deep? Bringing the shadows of darkness into the light is His specialty. Why in the world would we cheat God and limit His ability to bless us? It's time to launch out into deeper waters so that God can show Himself strong in our lives.

CHAPTER 3

FEAR NOT

"Fear not, for I have redeemed you; I have called you by your name; You are Mine. When you pass through the waters, I will be with you; and through the rivers, they shall not overflow you. When you walk through the fire, you shall not be burned, nor shall the flame scorch you. For I am the Lord your God, the Holy One of Israel, your Savior...

(Isaiah 43:1-3)

The phrase "fear not" appears sixty-three times in the King James Version of the Bible. It is amazing to realize that more emphasis is put on not fearing adverse circumstances than fearing the Lord Himself. We are admonished to fear God in Scripture about half the amount (thirty-two times) of times the word tells us to "fear not". Leaving fear at the front door as we leave to begin our day would appear to be a no-brainer, yet we need to keep the phrase "fear not" close to our hearts as we move through our day because of the constant adversity we find in our lives. It is mind-boggling how there are so many people who live their lives in constant fear. You would think that the warning Scripture gives about fear would make us more diligent in our seeking a way to avoid it at least, and at best learn how to overcome it.

When Scripture is misunderstood it has a tendency to bring with it a great amount of fear. Misinterpreting what God has to say is one of the main factors of ridding ourselves of this great weight, and consequently fear continues to dominate our lives. Case in point, let me leave you a Scripture that has many Christians running around in circles:

Therefore, if anyone is in Christ, he is a new creation; old things have passed away; behold, all things have become new.

(2 Corinthians 5:17)

Reality refutes that statement because there still are fleshly desires that control us each and every day. As much as we would like to believe the Scripture to be true in our lives, we must confess that we just don't measure up to the idealistic view of the Scripture. Coming to grips with that truth begins a domino effect of unbelief. Inside we begin to doubt the promises of God because if we cannot overcome in one of the most basic ways in serving God, how can we then accept the promises that will ensure us greater victory in the more difficult phases of the Christian life? If foundational truths cannot be accepted, then what does that say about our life in

Christ? That is frightening to admit, if not paralyzing, to say the least.

To work behind the scenes in the kingdom of God effectively, one must believe God when there are no physical evidences to back us up. When we take that stance, we are actually going against our better judgment because we have used "follow the evidence" as our mantra for success, and we live or die by it. When the evidence contradicts God's word, we must get to the point in our lives that we will believe God anyway.

Joseph's Incredible Dream

But while he thought about these things, behold, an angel of the Lord appeared to him in a dream, saying, "Joseph, son of David, do not be afraid to take to you Mary your wife, for that which is conceived in her is of the Holy Spirit. And she will bring forth a Son, and you shall call His name Jesus, for He will save His people from their sins."

(Matthew 1:20-21)

Joseph (Mary's husband) found himself in a dilemma that proves this point. The evidence actually pointed to the fact that Mary, his espoused wife, was an unfaithful woman. Explaining to Joseph what had happened was most difficult, because in reality it was unbelievable. To believe being pregnant without having sex was absurd, and this is the story that Mary was asking him to believe. As the relationship began to unravel, the Lord thought it necessary to send an angel Joseph's way to clear the air and confirm her story. Hearing it again did not make it any easier to accept, so God had to expand his understanding to set things straight.

These are the things that Joseph would have to consider and accept if this relationship with Mary was going to continue. First of all, he had to accept that the baby was conceived through the Holy Ghost and not another human being. Mary wasn't unfaithful to him, therefore he had no reason to reject her. This baby boy was chosen from amongst the Hebrew nation to become the promised Messiah, and just accepting that was almost as difficult as accepting Mary's virgin birth of the child. Lastly, the long-standing tradition of naming the first male child after the father was a no go. Because this baby had a call of God upon Him, it had already been decided in heaven what He would be named, and of course that name was Jesus.

It wasn't until I had become eligible to become a grandfather that I realized how important this naming tradition really is. As I go back now, I remember how when my son was born and I was asked of my father if we were going to name him George, which of course was his name as well. The disappointment on his face when I told him we had another name in mind still haunts me to this day. Now that my son is married and hopefully in the near future will have children, in the few discussions we have had about naming the child if it is a boy, the closest my name comes to him and his wife is perhaps using my name as a middle name. Now I know how my father felt, and I feel like I could identify with Joseph when that privilege of having a Junior was taken away from him. In his wisdom, Joseph decided to put his feelings aside, listen to the angel, and do the best he could to make Mary's pregnancy bearable without so much drama. They moved away from the city they lived in and waited patiently until the baby was born, to be able to move back to familiar surroundings.

"Fear not" is a common order we will hear from time to time in our walk with God. Because our obedience is faith-generated, we really don't have a right to question our orders no matter how unreasonable they may appear. Our responsibility is to take our orders and run with them until the task that is set before us has been completed. If and when God chooses to fill in the blanks, He will do so, and if not, all we have to come to grips with is that in this situation we were on a "need to know" basis.

When God's Response Time Is Slow

There will be times in our Christian experience that God will appear slower than molasses in responding to our petitions. Everything He does appears to have slowed down to a snail's crawl, and the temptation to take the bull by its horns and speed up the process is a temptation very difficult to avoid. The war for supremacy in the spirit world rages fiercely, and the enemy will take from us whatever we allow him to. When the decision not to oppose him comes to light, without even knowing it we give up our rights and settle in defeat. We must understand that more times than not, God will choose the time to accomplish His will. What is the virtue in this? The greatest virtue we will glean from our waiting on God is that it will allow Him to teach us patience.

My brethren, count it all joy when you fall into various trials, knowing that the testing of your faith produces patience.

(James 1:2-3)

41

Faith must be tested to grow, and as it grows it will produce patience. There is no way around it if you are to become dynamic in His kingdom. Having a great amount of patience does not make us passive in any way. To the contrary, the virtue of patience is shown in this Scripture:

> *But not a hair of your head shall be lost. By your patience possess your souls.*
>
> (Luke 21:18-19)

A lot of souls are being lost because of a lack of patience. Once our patience grows to a significant level it will open the door to greater trust in Him.

> *He has put a new song in my mouth. Praise to our God; Many will see it and fear, and will trust in the Lord.*
>
> (Psalm 40:3)

It is our trust in Him that will cause others to move in the same direction, and they too will know the Lord in the way He has always wanted.

When Daniel's Answer was Delayed

Daniel continued in a season of prayer, because when initially he touched the throne of God for an answer, there was none. He kept on coming back for the next twenty-one days, and even fasting could not hurry up God's response to this petition. His patience was put to the test as his faith was being molded and formed to do greater things for the kingdom of God. Finally Daniel received a response, an apology of sorts, from the throne of God.

Then he said to me, "Do not fear, Daniel, for from the first day that you set your heart to understand, and to humble yourself before your God, your words were heard; and I have come because of your words.

(Daniel 10:12)

His words were also heard by the enemy, and consequently a battle ensued in the spirit world. A demonic spirit was sent to make sure the message that Daniel was to receive was never delivered. That being said, it behooves me to warn anyone and everyone involved in spiritual warfare that our enemy is more than an adequate adversary. Remember, he has been at it for thousands of years, and with his experience knows how to fight, and even more so fight dirty. When Daniel finally broke through the spirit world, revelation came in abundance with the wisdom and authority few people knew.

The battles in the spiritual world continue to be ongoing. They are the reason for many delays in receiving answers to our petitions, but there is one truth that can never be dismissed in our experiences in spiritual warfare. We can be delayed an answer by Satan, but never can he deny us a response from God if our petitions are reaching the throne of glory on a daily basis.

For the weapons of our warfare are not carnal but mighty in God for pulling down strongholds, casting down arguments and every high thing that exalts itself against the knowledge of God, bringing every thought into captivity to the obedience of Christ

(2 Corinthians 10:4-5)

We needn't worry about bringing out the heavy artillery into our battles against Satan because our weaponry is maintained by God in the heavenlies. Our mindset and thought processes can be so fine-tuned that we have the ability to bring into captivity any and every thought to the obedience of Christ. In actuality, it is our choice not to live victoriously in Him, but if we choose to yield ourselves to Him unreservedly, then there is no devil this side of hell that can defeat us.

A Battle Reeking with Fear

It has been well documented in my previous books that my life has always been dominated by fear for as far as I can remember. It has been the root of all my insecurities, and being physically handicapped at times has hampered my personal relationships. When I was growing up, having a quiet spirit did not lend to great success in a Pentecostal environment. Even my decision not to continue my football career on the college level haunted me for years and emotionally stunted my growth in the things of the Lord. The fact that God was willing to take the time to teach me what faith was all about using baby steps was beyond my comprehension. He slowly and painfully took His time in molding me into what He wanted me to be. The process has taken more time than I care to admit to, nevertheless the process is ongoing after forty-one years of seeking His face.

After my bout with polio as a five-year-old, for the next forty-some odd years I never suffered any illnesses or pain in my body that required major medical attention. Unbeknownst to me in my childhood, when I got to my late fifties I was going to suffer a heart attack and stroke. Before that had an opportunity to occur, there were some other illnesses that I would have to overcome, both physically and emotionally. In 2010 at a routine doctor's visit, they found that I had an irregular heartbeat, my heart was beating out of rhythm. I was immediately advised to go to the hospital emergency room for further examination. It seemed ludicrous to me to spend money I did not have to pay for doctor's care, when in fact I didn't feel anything wrong with me. The fact of the matter was, with a little nudging from God I went. Long story short, I landed up having a catheter ablation procedure[6] that we would be charged over $90,000 for. Upon receiving the bill for the doctor's care and hospital stay, I said to myself, "There has to be a mistake. There's no way in the world I could have incurred that much of an expense in just three days." To my dismay, the bill was correct and I began to ponder on how I would be able to pay this.

My people are destroyed for lack of knowledge.

(Hosea 4:6)

Because we were unaware of the various charity programs that are available to low-income residents in Texas, we did not know that there were charity programs set up by the state to help those who did not have the financial resources to pay their bill. While we were in the hospital, no one came to us to offer that type of assistance, and it made for some pretty stressful times. Finally, after being released we were sent to an office to discuss the payment of the bill. It was then and there that we were made aware of a program in Texas that helped out people without health insurance. Again, without knowing how the system worked, in the back of my mind I was already seeing my life being turned upside down financially. Of course, the devil took advantage, terrorizing me at every moment, but I remembered a Scripture that had always worked for me, so I decided to use it again as I called upon the name of the Lord.

Call to Me, and I will answer you, and show you great and mighty things, which you do not know.

(Jeremiah 33:3)

If there was ever a time I was in the category of "I do not know what to do," it was then. But the little that I have learned in life has helped me to get along when adverse times have come my way. I've come to understand that that particular Scripture is true only if we put our faith to work. There are so many greater things God would like to provide in our lives, but He is limited in that these blessings are dependent upon our asking of Him. When signs and wonders became a normal part of my ministry, it was not because of the innate ability I had been born with. It had to do more with my consistency in seeking the face of God. Everything begins and ends in the presence of the King. He can't trust you with anything greater than what you have received if you are not willing to spend time with Him alone in His presence.

When God is in charge of your life, He will use anyone to come to your rescue. Whether they are saved or not, it really doesn't matter to Him. You don't have to believe me if you don't want to, but if you choose not to then you will have to rip out of the Bible the story of King Cyrus. He was the heathen king chosen by God to defeat the Babylonians. Once the Jewish nation was free of their bondage, it allowed them to go back to Jerusalem so that they could rebuild the Temple. Look at what Isaiah wrote about this particular heathen king. He was commissioned by God without even knowing it, and thinking that his brilliance was the determining factor of defeating one of the greatest nations in the world at that time. He never knew that God's hand was in it from the get-go. This is how Isaiah expressed King Cyrus' part in the overthrow of Babylon.

> *Who says of Cyrus, 'He is My shepherd, and he shall perform all My pleasure, Saying to Jerusalem, "You shall be built," and to the temple, "Your foundation shall be laid." Thus says the Lord to His anointed, to Cyrus, whose right hand I have held to subdue nations before him…*
>
> (Isaiah 44:28-45:1)

God chose Cyrus to do His dirty work and the king was led to believe that it was his genius and military know how that secured a victory over one of the greatest nations, if not the greatest in the world. He never came to the knowledge that the God of heaven was actually leading the charge of his army into victory. It is in instances like this that the Lord just blows me out of the water with His decisions. He is the God of glory, and yet there are times in Scripture that He defers credit to someone else just so that His will could be accomplished. If God has to go outside of His kingdom to provide for His children, He's not only willing but able as well.

A Personal Call to Us

God has always been a God of detail, so it's not surprising that He would take the time to call us personally by name. With God leading him, Adam was able to name each and every one of the animals in the Garden of Eden. To prove how meticulous God is in His care for us, He has written in His word that He even keeps track of every hair on our heads. You must understand that He doesn't count them, He actually numbers them. That makes it easier to understand the far-reaching effects of the love our God has for each and every one of us. Again, look at this Scripture that shows God's concern for the stars:

> *He counts the number of the stars; He calls them all by name.*

> (Psalm 147:4)

Doesn't it make sense that the Lord of glory is in it for the long haul and circumstances, failures, disappointments and the like are not great enough to allow Him to give up on us? He knows everything about us the good, the bad, and the ugly, yet He still loves us regardless.

The apostle Paul wrote a Scripture that can be taken two ways, from the believers' point of view and from His perspective.

> *For I am persuaded that neither death nor life, nor angels nor principalities nor powers, nor things present nor things to come, nor height nor depth, nor any other created thing, shall be able to separate us from the love of God which is in Christ Jesus our Lord.*

> (Romans 8:38-39)

It is a battle cry of sorts, a weapon in our arsenal that cannot be rendered useless. Anywhere, with anyone, at any time, will we be held hostage, in danger of going down in defeat. This is a rock solid guarantee that the Lord has got our back and our job in this is to hold on and trust Him until He gets us out of our mess.

On the other hand, Jesus also has a responsibility to be there if and when we call on His name. There are no misunderstandings or misinterpreting the job that needs to be done. He is completely dedicated to bringing our negative situation to a peaceful solution. Most of all, He does all of this with pleasure.

> *Let them shout for joy and be glad, who favor my righteous cause; and let them say continually, "Let the Lord be magnified, who has pleasure in the prosperity of His servant."*
>
> (Psalm 35:27)

There should be a continual shout of joy in our hearts for the great promises the Lord has given. He is not a mean, unjust God, as some paint Him to be, but rather a giving God who takes pleasure in the prosperity of His servants. You could almost say that with each and every blessing given out to His children, there are goose bumps that run all through His body.

> *...In Your presence is fullness of joy; at Your right hand are pleasures forevermore.*
>
> (Psalm 16:11)

His right hand in Scripture has always been the hand of provision. Realizing that He is not a stingy God, we have every right to approach His throne with boldness, expecting the best that heaven has to offer. Our job is to put our faith to work and watch the hand of God move mightily in our lives. That's doable, don't you think? If that is true, and surely it is, "Fear Not" is doable in all our lives.

> ...*Fear not, for I have redeemed you; I have called you by your name; You are Mine.*
>
> (Isaiah 43:1)

The Lord is calling our name, can you hear it?

CHAPTER 4

HIDDEN COSTS

For which of you, intending to build a tower, does not sit down first and count the cost, whether he has enough to finish it lest, after he has laid the foundation, and is not able to finish, all who see it begin to mock him, saying, 'This man began to build and was not able to finish.'

(Luke 14:28-30)

Constructing your dream home is a major effort, if anything at all. It could take months and even years in the planning stages if all is done right. A wise builder will take into consideration the hidden costs that are common in every building project. These costs are usually unexpected and cannot be specifically planned for. Depending on what part of the country you live in, inclement weather delays can become a nuisance if the contractor has not budgeted for this time loss. There will be times that materials are out of stock and an order must be placed with companies that are further away and the distance adds to the time. On occasion when they are available, errors are made in shipping and it only delays the process even more. Anyone who has had any kind of experience in construction knows that at various times you will encounter legalistic building inspectors who are rigid in their approval of your building project. You could almost swear up and down that they have it out for you, but in reality they treat everyone the same way. These hidden costs can literally be buried underground where faulty foundations are discovered, tree roots take their toll, bursting pipes in the plumbing, and even the best cared for buildings have had termites weakening the structure by whittling away the wood frame that is hidden to the naked eye itself.

To compensate for these hidden costs, one must be flexible in estimating time involved and money to be spent. Delays for whatever reasons are a normal cost of doing business and adjustments are made to include the unexpected. I remember talking to a pastor at one time, who started a building program. He had allowed tens of thousands of dollars more added to an extra six months of construction time. In the end, that was not enough, and consequently the building program was halted until more funds could be raised and made available to this building project. Controlling delays by overestimating construction time not only shows the wisdom of the person in charge, it also demonstrates the experience of a successful contractor. Nothing catches him off guard, and if by any chance it does, he's been around the block many times before and knows not to fret, for somehow, some way, the job will get completed.

We can take these lessons learned in construction and apply them in our spiritual battles we fight daily. The losses incurred in this realm could lead to an eternal destiny without God, and therefore strict attention must be allotted so that a life will not be lost eternally because of our carelessness. That is a loss that we all will not be able to recover from, and consequently needless to say. The suffering needed to endure in the Christian life is a hidden cost worth the trouble, knowing that the result in the end will produce His glory. God's glory to be produced in us will be priceless.

Consider the Sufferings

For I consider that the sufferings of this present time are not worthy to be compared with the glory which shall be revealed in us.

(Romans 8:18)

Considering the suffering a Christian is asked to endure is another way of "counting the cost." Because of that fact, we are willing to do everything in our power to obtain that glory. I just recently came to understand this revelation given to me referring to His glory. The glory of God revealed in us doesn't have to wait till eternity. I have learned that when suffering has run its course, the glory of God is then released into our lives. The apostle Paul says this in so many words as he wrote to the Corinthians in chapter 3 of 2 Corinthians.

But we all, with unveiled face, beholding as in a mirror the glory of the Lord, are being transformed into the same image from glory to glory, just as by the Spirit of the Lord.

(2 Corinthians 3:18)

The unveiling of His glory makes us more like Him. The full benefit of His glory includes a godly image here on earth. If that be true, and we know that God is not a liar, then why are we so dissatisfied with what God has to offer? Are we so heavenly minded that we have deferred a heaven on earth mindset to the time we spend eternity in His presence? Why wait till we get to glory when we can have heaven here on earth? I believe that the pursuit of His glory here on earth should be done at any cost.

> *"Again, the kingdom of heaven is like treasure hidden in a field, which a man found and hid; and for joy over it he goes and sells all that he has and buys that field.*
>
> (Matthew 13:44)

To the casual observer, this man has paid way too much, opening himself up to harsh criticism. In the aftermath, this man is considered a shrewd businessman, one who foresaw this hidden wealth and sacrificed everything for it. The sacrifices that we make here on earth will truly have eternal benefits as we make our way to heaven.

When I chose to serve God at the tender age of seventeen, it brought harsh criticism from all sides. Coaches, family, and friends alike took their turn in berating my decision, and literally I had no place to hide. Leaving behind a football scholarship to USC, and potentially a pro career, did not make any sense to anyone who knew me. I could not reconcile putting God to one side and playing a meaningless game instead of serving the God who had willingly given up His life that I might have salvation. What ultimately would be the profit?

> *For what profit is it to a man if he gains the whole world, and loses his own soul? Or what will a man give in exchange for his soul? For the Son of Man will come in*

*the glory of His Father with His angels, and then He will
reward each according to his works.*

(Matthew 16:26-27)

The temporary joy found in playing a game could not
compensate for the eternal joy that would be found in
serving the Lord. The hidden benefit, of course, was that
I would not have to wait to reach glory in heaven to
experience it here on earth. The Scripture above says
that we will be rewarded according to our works. That
being said, it behooves us to put a concerted effort into
our service unto the Lord. The benefits are not only
heavenly, they are so far beyond our comprehension we
can't even imagine what they will be.

Hidden Costs Are a Normal Part of Business

It is to our advantage to understand that hidden costs
are a normal part of doing business in His kingdom. In
actuality, it is God's way of procuring blessings in our
lives that are not available to those who do not serve
Him in spirit and in truth. The apostle Paul truly
understood the point that I am trying to make in that he
was completely sold out to the Master.

When Saul of Tarsus was called to the ministry, this
call was to be predicated on suffering. Unbeknownst to
him (now known as Paul after his conversion), there
were others to whom God took the time to reveal just
how much this former enemy of the gospel would have
to endure physically, emotionally, and spiritually.

*But the Lord said to him (Ananias), "Go, for he is a
chosen vessel of Mine to bear My name before Gentiles,*

kings, and the children of Israel. For I will show him how many things he must suffer for My name's sake."

(Acts 9:15-16)

It has always been God's M.O. to bring along His children slowly. He has successfully used the "need to know basis" to enhance His kingdom. God is aware that His grace is sufficient to bring about success in any area, with anyone, at any time, to the point that He will ask His children to trust Him when He has asked us to do something without explanation.

To the outsider, the Lord's tactics appear self-serving and heartless. To the contrary, hiding the cost of serving Him was to Paul's benefit. Not knowing what came next helped control the torment of fear, thus freeing him to do the work of the Lord without apprehension. It was done for his own good to get the most out of his call that could not be accomplished by just any man. Bringing the salvation plan to the Gentiles was to be difficult enough without fear hindering the process. Hiding his sorrows would be the most efficient way to maximize his call from God.

An Impossible Request

Daniel found himself in a dilemma one day that would not be easily solved. Babylon was in a tizzy over King Nebuchadnezzar's threat. Many believed that he had lost his mind because of the demand that he was making of his magicians. He was ordering any one of them to interpret a dream he had without knowing what the dream was. If no one was able to interpret that dream, then all the wise men in Nebuchadnezzar's kingdom would die, including Daniel. Exposing the hidden cost (i.e., the dream) would be impossible for the magicians. This impossibility allowed Daniel to operate in his gift. We must understand the mind of God in that He is willing to equip us for success in times of need.

I will give you the treasures of darkness and hidden riches of secret places that you may know that I, the Lord, who call you by your name, am the God of Israel.

(Isaiah 45:3)

The authenticity of our God will be verified when He gives us the treasures of darkness and hidden riches of secret places. Signs and wonders will become commonplace to our ministries and nothing will be hidden from heaven so that we will be most effective here on earth.

Sheltered in the Arms of God

When we were planning our first trip to New York in 2012, it needed to be planned well and efficiently (cost-effective), because as you all well know, visiting New York can be very costly. Although most of our ministry would be directed towards the Queens area, hotel costs were more than we were willing to pay. In actuality, because the pastors who had agreed to let us visit were going to foot the bill, we didn't want to be a financial burden to these congregations. We settled in Spring Valley, which was about ninety minutes away, more or less, from the various churches we had been programmed to speak in. We were willing to take on the added expense of time and gasoline so that we could be more of a blessing to those who received our ministry. On the last day of our trip, Hurricane Sandy ravaged the area, devastating everything in its path. As I was finishing ministry that day, we received the final evacuation warning on our phone. We finished ministering just in time, because shortly after we left and arrived at our hotel, the hurricane began to damage the area completely. I had never felt hurricane gusts of wind as powerful as I felt them that day, and only because the hotel chosen was on higher ground we were able to escape the flooding. Truth be told, it was like we were protected from the fierce winds and inclement weather, and in our eyes at the time it was just another storm. When news got out as to the damage that was done, it was hard to imagine they were talking about the same storm we had just experienced. It wasn't until days later, as we were driving out of New York through New Jersey, that we were able to comprehend with our own eyes the damage Sandy had created with such ferocity. The electricity in our hotel never went out like most hotels in our area, and we were able to leave New York a couple of days later without a scratch. Because we were willing to spend more time and money (i.e., hidden costs), God was willing to reveal His secrets to protect us from the storm.

> *He reveals deep and secret things; He knows what is in the darkness, and light dwells with Him.*
>
> (Daniel 2:22)

We did not have to wait like everyone else to find out where the hurricane was going to hit hardest. God was willing to take the time and warned us to keep us out of danger. Our trip was cut a day short, the day that had been designated for sightseeing. In reality, I don't think anyone during that time was able to have that luxury. I'm just thankful to God that He was able to reveal the secret things that kept us out of harm's way.

Special Treasure

Sad to say, recognizing hidden costs is not enough to remedy the situation. A strategy must be put into action for the hidden cost not to slow down the project, or even worse, stop it completely.

> *Therefore, to him who knows to do good and does not do it, to him it is sin.*
>
> (James 4:17)

The Scripture above is one of those that really put our service to God in perspective. We will not be judged solely on the things that we do, but also in determining our judgment, we will be judged for not doing the things we knew were right and good. If we are willing to risk it all, there is a special promise given to us that will guarantee a positive outcome, one perhaps we do not deserve.

> *Now therefore, if you will indeed obey My voice and keep My covenant, then you shall be a special treasure to Me above all people; for all the earth is Mine.*
>
> (Exodus 19:5)

With all of the earth at His disposal, it really says something that God would consider us a special treasure. The world does not even look twice at our accomplishments, much less our relationship with God. Yet we can rest assured that our God is tickled to death over the fact that He owns something special that He is not so easily willing to give up. Everywhere we go, when I tell testimonies like this the response I get from those listening is amazing. Most want to experience the same things, yet are not willing to pay those hidden costs.

"Thus says the Lord of hosts: 'In those days ten men from every language of the nations shall grasp the sleeve of a Jewish man, saying, "Let us go with you, for we have heard that God is with you."'"

(Zechariah 8:23)

They are willing to search for the deeper things in God if it will not cost too much. They seem to have the same attitude that the young rich ruler had when he approached Jesus one day with a question.

Now a certain ruler asked Him, saying, "Good Teacher, what shall I do to inherit eternal life?"

(Luke 18:18)

The response from Jesus was not quite what this rich young ruler was expecting. In the past, he was willing to give from what was left over, but what God was asking was going to cost him a little too much.

So when Jesus heard these things, He said to him, "You still lack one thing. Sell all that you have and distribute to the poor, and you will have treasure in heaven; and come, follow Me."

(Luke 18:22)

Jesus hit him where it hurt the most, his riches. Giving them up to follow Him would be a cost he believed he could not bear.

I Want a Ministry Like Yours

It amuses me when I hear people say they would love to have a ministry much like the one God has given to me. Little do they know the pain and suffering, not to mention the sacrifices my wife and I make to be a blessing to others, which comes at a high price. We are on the road for three months at a time before we have to return home for medical checkups. We miss holidays, birthdays and anniversaries, we rarely go to weddings, and we have even missed some funerals. We have never seen our only grandchild walk, and to tell you the truth, he probably doesn't even recognize us after being away from him for such a long time. Yet all of this is part of being mightily used of God.

Our Willingness to Pay Hidden Costs

Our willingness to pay hidden costs can lead to hidden treasure. We never know when we are going to have our faith challenged, so we must be ready for anything that comes our way. We are originally from the West Coast, actually born and raised in Southern California. We now make our home in Texas, about 1,500 miles away from friends and family. We make it a point to visit our old stomping grounds at least once a year. This trip extends to at least a month of ministry, if not more. Because the weather is so heavenly, it makes it extremely easy to spend time in the Golden State. A couple of years ago, I was able to program a trip to Oregon that would take up at least two weeks of our summer. Instead of flying to the West Coast, I made arrangements with the pastor bringing us to Oregon to pay for our gasoline expense instead. We had gone to California a week or so before our ministry in Oregon would begin. Of course, my wife and I took advantage of being able to visit with family and friends we had known for many years before moving to Texas. Of course, eating real Mexican food was such a delight that I almost did not want to leave, but duty called. The day before we were to leave for Oregon, I got ahold of the sponsoring pastor to confirm our visit, but in trying to reach him, I actuality got his secretary instead, who informed me that the revival services planned had been canceled, with no reschedule in mind. The pastor's brother had been tragically killed in an auto accident, and of course the time and money reserved for our revival services would be instead used to pay for the funeral. I was so tempted to stay in California for the simple reason that in times past we had bonded with many pastors of different Jesus' name organizations. It had gotten to the point that I felt confident, even at the last minute, that I could fill my calendar for the next three weeks without a problem. It was at that time the Lord spoke to me and said to go to Oregon anyway. In the back of my mind, I knew that God could provide for us financially, even if I went to an area where my ministry was not known. In actuality, the problem was personal in that I did not want to be put in a position where I was begging people I did not know for an opportunity to minister. A lesson of trust I had learned long ago had been brought back to my attention, and thus the decision was made to make our way to Oregon just like God had asked.

A Lesson That Never Gets Old
Humble yourselves in the sight of the Lord, and He will lift you up.

(James 4:10)

Anything can be accomplished if people are willing to humble themselves before the Lord. God was not only trying to stir up my faith, but also had a great blessing in store for me as well. I methodically began to make my phone calls to men I had never met, but because of the circumstances of my phone call and they knowing the pastor in their area who had suffered the loss, they were willing to take a chance on a man of God they did not know and had never heard preach before. My calling of these pastors could be put under the category of "cold calls," because I did not know any of them. The grace of the Lord had truly fallen upon me in that even the district superintendent of the area was willing to take a chance on a man he knew nothing about. It did not hurt that he actually had gone to Bible school with a younger sister of mine, and I believe that opened the doors to his church. He was then willing to help schedule other pastors in the area so that I could stick around for the next two weeks at least. Twenty-three days later, I had spoken in eighteen different services and fifteen of those services were in churches I had never spoken in before. Even a district conference celebrated during this time could not put a damper on the invitations, although the conference did lessen the amount I spoke one week because all the churches had shut down for the conference. This truly was another lesson God wanted to teach me about trusting Him to provide when all looked lost, one of the lessons that will not be easily forgotten.

What will you do in the Lord when confronted with hidden costs? Will they drive you away from God's blessing, or will you allow God the opportunity to bless your life? The decision rests in your hands.

CHAPTER 5

IN DANGER OF
LOSING OUR ONENESS

"Hear, O Israel: The Lord our God, the Lord is one! You shall love the Lord your God with all your heart, with all your soul, and with all your strength.

(Deuteronomy 6:4-5)

If the foundations are destroyed, what can the righteous do?

(Psalm 11:3)

From the birth of the Oneness Pentecostal doctrine, life in the mainstream Christian world has not been pleasant because in most circles we are considered the unwanted stepchild. With the same fervor of dislike (sometimes even hate), Oneness Pentecostals and the rest of the Christian world just do not get along. We have been criticized, much to the chagrin of each and every member, that at times bringing the two factions together is nearly impossible.

Similar to the Arabs and Jews

That being said, any Oneness Pentecostal who has come from the other side knows from personal experience just how misunderstood our doctrine can be. Dogmatic believers on both sides take their verbal jabs at each other with the intent of defending their faith, hoping that they will eventually connect and knock out their opponent. I have read somewhat vicious conversations posted on blogs on various Internet sites. Without resorting to the use of foul language, they sure have come close, using abusive language that comes pretty close to something you would hear in a bar.

The only thing that is truly wrong about our Oneness presentation is the presentation itself and the attitude it is being presented in. There has to be a defense of the gospel, but it must be presented in a Christ-like manner. But the dislike that each side has for the other almost can be compared to that of the Jews and Arabs. The Arab world badly outnumbers the nation of Israel, yet in past history the Arabs have not been able to destroy God's people. The challenge that is being waved in our face is similar to the challenge David encountered when he chose to fight Goliath. The giant from Gath was undefeated in all his fights, and the challenger before him would not pose a threat. But there are strange things that can happen "in the name of the Lord" that would have even the greatest of warriors running for cover. It is with that type of spirit we, as Oneness Pentecostals, should defend our faith. We must be like the Scripture has said:

"Behold, I send you out as sheep in the midst of wolves. Therefore be wise as serpents and harmless as doves.

(Matthew 10:16)

Our Future Existence Hangs on This

Our future existence is dependent upon our ability to defend the Oneness doctrine, yet there are other truths revealed unto us that must be treasured just as diligently. The Mount Rushmore of success in the Lord is actually three-pronged. These are the three doctrines that we must be willing to uphold and never change: Oneness doctrine, receiving the Holy Ghost evidenced by speaking in other tongues, and living a life in Holiness.

Though one may be overpowered by another, two can withstand him. And a threefold cord is not quickly broken.

(Ecclesiastes 4:12)

The one God doctrine is based on many Scriptures, but for the sake of brevity I will mention the Scripture where this doctrine has been founded.

Then Peter said to them, "Repent, and let every one of you be baptized in the name of Jesus Christ for the remission of sins; and you shall receive the gift of the Holy Spirit. For the promise is to you and to your children, and to all who are afar off, as many as the Lord our God will call."

(Acts 2:38-39)

This is where salvation is found and is considered the cornerstone of the Oneness doctrine.

To strengthen our position, we must add to the foundation the doctrine of the baptism of the Holy

Ghost. This is applied when the believer receives the Spirit of God, with evidence of speaking in other tongues. Upon receiving this wonderful gift from on high, every believer is promised God's power from above.

> *But you shall receive power when the Holy Spirit has come upon you; and you shall be witnesses to Me in Jerusalem, and in all Judea and Samaria, and to the end of the earth."*
>
> (Acts 1:8)

It is truly incredible what God is doing through the moving of His Spirit. With His glory being released in each and every service, signs and wonders have the opportunity to flow unrestricted. More and more Oneness Pentecostals are coming to grips with this promise, and in applying it to their personal lives they are watching God move in miraculous ways.

> *Finally, my brethren, be strong in the Lord and in the power of His might. Put on the whole armor of God, that you may be able to stand against the wiles of the devil.*
>
> (Ephesians 6:10-11)

Speaking in tongues is only one of the benefits one receives when the baptism of the Holy Ghost is pursued. The onslaught against the devil is intensified with the power of His might working miraculously in His strength. We needn't worry about the outcome of our spiritual battles because it is He who is fighting, not only with us, but for us as well.

Our foundation would not be complete without our service to Him in Holiness. This attribute is so important that the author of Hebrews took the time to write to us that... *without which no man shall see the Lord* (Hebrews 12:14). The Lord thought it so important to serve Him in Holiness that He not only made it a requirement to enter into heaven, but also extended that command to include both inward and outward appearance. Any Christian who serves Him with one and not the other is truly falling short. If a person honestly and wholeheartedly loves the Lord, it will begin on the inside (what God sees) but it will to extend itself to our outward appearance (what man sees) as well.

Divide and Conquer

It is with this foundational truth that Satan prepares his attacks against the true Christian who serves God in all three areas. He continues to use a time-tested weapon that has been successful throughout the ages, and that being said, there is no reason for him to alter his barrage of attacks. The form of attack he uses most successfully is the one to "divide and conquer." With an astute strategy formed to render each and every Pentecostal helpless, Satan first attacks the Holiness standard of the Church. Of all the doctrines the Church must adhere to, the Holiness doctrine is its weakest link. When all that we believe is placed for the world to see, the doctrine most varied in interpretation is the honoring of our Holiness standard. I have had the opportunity to travel throughout the entire United States and parts of Mexico, Central and South America. I can go to pretty much any part of the world in our organization, and if I enter into a service blindfolded, not knowing where I am in particular, I can pretty much figure it out when the blindfold is removed and I look into the crowd. There are always varying degrees of what "modest apparel" looks like, and because of the wide range of interpretation it has caused a lot of dissension amongst the various factions.

The subtle assault to destroy the Church begins when that dissension rears its ugly head over the different interpretations of what "Holiness" should be. The quickest and most effective way this attack can be successful in dividing the Church is to begin to attack our women. Appealing to a woman's emotions has always been a powerful and proven way to allow Satan's accusations to cause doubt. It proved to be a successful weapon in the Garden of Eden when Satan, through the serpent, appealed to Eve's emotions. If she had not been drawn away by her own lust (to be like God), chances are Satan would have had to find another way to dismantle God's plan.

A Most Effective Weapon: Half-Truths

The unraveling of the truth began as Satan, the ultimate deceiver, convinced Eve to disregard God's word by using half-truths.

> *Then the serpent said to the woman, "You will not surely die. For God knows that in the day you eat of it your eyes will be opened, and you will be like God, knowing good and evil."*

> (Genesis 3:4-5)

The death Satan was mentioning was true because he was trying to get Eve to focus completely on the physical. What he was hoping to accomplish, and he did successfully, was to deceive Eve in disobeying God's command so that a spiritual death would occur. She was presumptuous in believing that being like God was a good thing and would only make their lives in the garden more fruitful. What she did not consider, and probably had no way of really knowing, was that disobedience to the word of God had consequences.

The Lord decided to visit His creation one day in the garden and called out to them. In the past, whatever they were doing was put aside to give their complete attention to the Lord. This time around, He found them hiding in the bushes and in all seriousness wanted to know why.

> *Then the eyes of both of them were opened, and they knew that they were naked; and they sewed fig leaves together and made themselves covering.*
>
> (Genesis 3:7)

Their act of disobedience was a pure form of presumption (it will be discussed in later chapters) at its finest. Eve was convinced that being like God by eating the forbidden fruit was a good thing and was able to convince Adam as well. Up to that point in their experience with God, everything was done as He had asked. There was no way for them to know, nor to understand what the consequences of disobedience would be.

Up to this point their obedience to every word of God not only brought security, but peace of mind as well. After their act of disobedience, for the first time in their lives they felt fear and its consequences. Their disobedience to the commandment of God would bring judgment into their lives for the first time. What they thought they were giving up in the very beginning by allowing God to have complete control was nowhere near as painful as the judgment that God pronounced on them. When the Lord found them both hiding and being fully clothed, it saddened the Lord when forced to pronounce judgment. In reality, they were not naked like Adam had proclaimed, because from the very beginning the glory of God had clothed them. In essence, they made a decision to trade the glory of God for fig leaves. What was even worse was the banishment of them both from the Garden of Eden.

His Tactics Haven't Changed

The same tactic used to deceive Eve in the Garden is the same one he uses on us today. Satan will try to infiltrate the minds of our ladies, speaking half-truths if not lies themselves, to begin crumbling the importance of keeping a modest outward appearance. With subtle hints, he begins to suggest that this particular way of dress is completely antiquated and out of date. This way of dress is also chauvinistic as well, and is forced upon our ladies to keep them under wraps. The most difficult objection to refute in the most part is when our ladies try to make their case by saying, "If the way that I dress is so bad, then why does God still bless me?"

Or do you despise the riches of His goodness, forbearance, and longsuffering, not knowing that the goodness of God leads you to repentance?

(Romans 2:4)

God is not blessing the female gender because He approves of their ways, it is more so that He is willing to overlook your faults in the meantime, as He has the opportunity to lead us to a better and more perfect way. There is a spiritual significance attached to modest dress, and I would like to spend some time explaining that significance.

A Spiritual Significance

The Old Testament prophets wore a mantle that had a spiritual significance attached to it. It was not only unique in its appearance, but the spiritual aspects of the mantle set it apart from all the others. It was bulky and rugged looking, so that the elements would not affect the prophet in any way to minister unto the people effectively. Taking these characteristics into consideration, they can be applied to the Christian and his walk with God in Holiness.

The mantle of holiness is first of all the identification to the world that we have been separated onto God. The Old Testament prophet could be immediately identified without even opening his mouth. This was so because his mantle spoke to the rest of the world of his special calling of God. On the other hand, the Old Testament prophet used his mantle to protect himself from the elements of the weather, while we use our spiritual mantle to protect us from seducing spirits. The covering will protect the anointing of the Holy Ghost living inside of us. It is essential to keep this mantle on so that seducing spirits would not steer us to false doctrines that are popping up more frequently in the times in which we live.

Now the Spirit speaketh expressly, that in the latter times some shall depart from the faith, giving heed to seducing spirits, and doctrines of devils;

(1 Timothy 4:1)

No one can deny that we are now living in the latter times. False doctrines are sprouting up everywhere at an alarming rate. The most dangerous words are produced by people possessed by seducing spirits. They are charismatic in their personality, drawing multitudes of people with their watered-down version of the gospel. There are no sinners, and defining sin itself is left up to that group's leader. It is what he or she decides that determines what the followers will believe. It is that type of leadership that lends itself to gross sin, and because they are somewhat dictatorial in their leadership style, no one can steer them away from their beliefs.

A Classic Example of Seducing Spirits

Back in the late 1970s, an event happened that shocked the world. Rev. Jim Jones was an American religious leader and community organizer who founded the People's Temple. He was best known as the leader for the cult murder/suicide in 1978 of 909 of his members in Jonestown, Guyana. Over 300 children were murdered at Jonestown, almost all of them by cyanide poisoning. Jones died from a gunshot wound to the head; to this day it is unknown whether his death was a suicide or murder.

His life and death were classic examples of seducing spirits overpowering a man who, in the beginning, had a true call from God. Their influence was so strong that he lived a life of contradiction. On one hand, he preached homosexuality was a sin. On the other hand, he was arrested in 1973 and charged with soliciting a man for sex in a movie theater bathroom. On one hand, Jones banned sex among Temple members outside of marriage, while on the other hand he himself engaged in sexual relations with both male and female Temple members. In one of those relations he fathered a son, Jim Jon. His drug of choice was morphine, and of course he abused it greatly. His paranoia of his ministry being taken away was what finally put him over the top. With a calm assurance, he convinced most of his followers to commit "revolutionary suicide" with him. This resulted in the greatest single loss of American civilian life any deliberate act until the September 11, 2001 attacks.[7]

If there ever was a case of "seducing spirits" causing a man to lose his mind, it was this one. One thing led to another, opening himself up to voices that were not of God. The end result was a tragedy beyond belief. The power of "seducing spirits" is incredible.

Now it's time to move on to the second rung of foundational truths, that being our praise and worship. The great revival of God's Spirit moving amongst His people has increased steadily in the 21st century. The freedom that we have as Christians to praise and worship our God has skyrocketed upward compared to prior generations. For the first time in years, there appears to be a consensus on how the name of the Lord should be praised with vibrant expressions from the heart. The church mouse of today is no longer quiet (if he's Pentecostal, that is). The noise sent up from our sanctuaries can at times be heard from the street, and it is a joyful noise at that.

How Satan Manipulates Our Praise

One of the things we must concern ourselves with, as we draw closer to the Lord, is how Satan will try to manipulate our praise and worship so that we might not get the best God has to offer. In the past he has used our gifts against us, and seeing that that method had a lot of success, he continues to keep us away from God's best, short-circuiting the blessings from heaven. Because he's aware that the moving of God's Spirit in our worship opens the door to the supernatural, it gives him the opportunity once again to use "seducing spirits" to confound us. As unfair as it would appear to be, using our weapons against us, it just doesn't seem right. This is where the use of our mantle comes in. As previously stated, the mantle God has equipped us with, will protect us from those deceiving spirits. As long as our holiness (both in and out) is put on, there is no devil this side of hell that can seduce us. If we find ourselves in that situation, it's only because we have allowed the enemy to come in.

In every church service, Satan is not so concerned whether we can praise and worship our way to victory. There is no way he can stop the power of God from falling if the saints of God are willing to worship the Lord in spirit and in truth. What he does, conniving us, is he waits for the moving of God's Spirit to subside and then he has an opportunity to steal our victory by sending seducing spirits our way to confuse us. It is a very successful tactic in that without spiritual protection of the mantle, it is open season on us. That being said, we must come to the conclusion that "modest dress" is more than just a rule and regulation. In actuality, it will ward off evil spirits at a time that we are most vulnerable. There have been countless times in the past that after a glorious outpouring of God's spirit has saturated the entire sanctuary, the next day there are reports of young people who had fallen into sin just moments after that glorious experience. Why did that occur? Because there was no spiritual protection for them and they were unable to discern the voices and or feelings registering in their minds and hearts, and consequently made bad decisions.

The Battle Becomes More Fierce

Once the two foundational truths are done away with, Satan has a direct line to work on the third and most important truth. He will do his best to sabotage our belief in the Oneness doctrine that God has revealed to us. When the first two truths have been compromised by our newfound beliefs, it will then become far easier for him to convince us to leave our most important belief, the Oneness of God.

In the book of Revelation we find the documentation of the seven churches of Asia Minor. One of those churches had a proud heritage in that they were very zealous for the name of Jesus.

> *"And to the angel of the church in Pergamos write, 'These things says He who has the sharp two-edged sword: "I know your works, and where you dwell, where Satan's throne is. And you hold fast to My name, and did not deny My faith even in the days in which Antipas was My faithful martyr, who was killed among you, where Satan dwells. But I have a few things against you, because you have there those who hold the doctrine of Balaam, who taught Balak to put a stumbling block before the children of Israel, to eat things sacrificed to idols, and to commit sexual immorality. Thus you also have those who hold the doctrine of the Nicolaitans, which thing I hate.*
>
> (Revelation 2:12-15)

Pergamos is infamous in Scripture in that they were a very "sensual church." They were also out of God's will by following the error of Baalam (i.e., greed and lust). Adultery and fornication were running rampant through the streets of Pergamos, and no one appeared to have the desire to set things in order. Their mantra was, "If it feels good, do it." Their saving grace was the fact that they were willing to diligently hold on to the name of Jesus. As these spirits began to take complete control, they were able to attack the next foundational doctrine, which was the receiving of the baptism of the Holy Ghost evidenced by speaking in other tongues. Their belief in receiving the spirit of God never changed. What did change, however, was how that gift was to be received and maintained. As seducing spirits took control of the Pergamos church, speaking in tongues was no longer considered the initial evidence that the Spirit of God had been received. Added to their beliefs was this philosophy. The Spirit is dead, the name of Jesus is no longer important, but the search for knowledge is now paramount to our success in God.

It did not take centuries for a change of philosophy to manifest itself in Pergamos. They still considered themselves religious people, yet their religion was now based more on what they believed it to be rather than what God had established. When man feels he is in control of his own destiny, it is a major sign that the judgment of God is not far behind. Why? This is true because humanity will be left to their own understanding, a decision that will ultimately end in disaster.

The battle for our soul rages on and continues to intensify. Time is getting short before the final judgment and Satan is hopelessly condemned to his final destination; i.e., hell. Our spiritual foundations were designed to ultimately protect us from such panic attacks. Our foundations have started to crumble, and once they are destroyed, everything else will crumble as well.

If the foundations are destroyed, what can the righteous do?

(Psalm 11:3)

Once they are gone, they will be gone forever. Can we really take that chance?

CHAPTER 6

PRESUMPTUOUS SINS

Keep back Your servant also from presumptuous sins; Let them not have dominion over me. Then I shall be blameless, and I shall be innocent of great transgression.

(Psalm 19:13)

I am sure that at one time or another, you have heard the word presumption or presumptuous, but if I were to ask what in detail does it mean, I'm sure that I would receive a number of blank stares. Since the next three chapters in one way or another will deal with this subject, it behooves us to give a definition to help us all stay on the same page. Webster says that a person that is presumptuous is one that is *being too confident: something done or made without permission, right, or good reason, overstepping bounds and taking liberties.*[8] From the get-go we must get something straight. **PRESUMPTION** is not **FAITH**, neither does it have any place in the faith discussion. It has subtly knocked faith to the floor and is determined not to let it get back up. What is the difference between the two, you might ask? Faith is released when God gives us a command and we obey it as instructed. It is always God-initiated, therefore God has an obligation to bring it to pass. Presumption, on the other hand, is nothing more than a good idea that is humanly initiated. It could in some instances bring great blessing, but truth be told a person is gambling with his life and/or ministry when the reason for doing something good in God's kingdom is presumptuous at the core. It is so despised by God that by avoiding it, one can be innocent of great transgression.

Satan has devised a diabolical plan to substitute faith with presumption. Why is he so confident that his weapon of choice will be so successful? It was the same error he committed as one of God's top angels, Lucifer. Presumption made him believe that he could ascend to the throne of God and be just as powerful as the Lord Himself. He has continued throughout the ages to use this weapon effectively, and when anyone takes the bait, the results are always disastrous.

The effect of this error is the same as when wheat and tares are confused with each other. They are both so similar in appearance that it is hard to tell the difference between the two. Wheat has the ability, when eaten correctly, to bring strength to our bodies. Tares, on the other hand, look very similar to wheat, but eating it will cause sickness. When a work is carried out presumptuously, God is not obligated to answer our petition no matter how noble it may appear. If what we are attempting in the kingdom of God is not God-initiated, He cannot be forced to comply. We might get a positive answer from time to time, but more times than not it will end up in failure and consequently cause irreparable damage. That is why our stepping out by faith in times past has been so iffy, sometimes it worked and sometimes it didn't. Presumption makes answers to prayers so unpredictable that we come to the conclusion that it is a waste of time because there is an enormous chance you will not receive a positive result from God anyway, so why even try? It's really not worth the trouble.

Cain and Abel

The story we find in the Bible of two brothers, Cain and Abel, is a story replete with presumption. When the orders from heaven came down, both men were asked to offer sacrifices onto their God. It was the custom at that time to offer an animal sacrifice, but only Abel complied with God's order. In preparing his sacrifice, Cain believed that if he offered God the best from his garden it would be sufficient to satisfy God's request. It was clearly a presumptuous mistake on his part, because replacing a blood sacrifice with a sacrifice of food did not meet the blood requirements God demanded in all sacrifices onto Him. I'm sure Cain must have thought, "What's the big deal? They are just going to be burnt up by the fire anyway; the results would turn out to be the same." He presumed that the sacrifice was just a ritual and had no spiritual significance. As it turned out, this blood sacrifice was only a preview of the ultimate shedding of blood at Calvary. There was an important truth that Cain had completely discarded when he made his substituted offering.

And according to the law almost all things are purified with blood, and without shedding of blood there is no remission.

(Hebrews 9:22)

His presumption caused his sacrifice to be rejected by God and his bitterness resulted in the murder of his brother, Abel. It also led him to believe he too, along with his sacrifice, was being rejected by the same God. His presumptuous sin caused a more harsh judgment than he could bear.

And He (God) said, "What have you done? The voice of your brother's blood cries out to Me from the ground. So now you are cursed from the earth, which has opened its mouth to receive your brother's blood from your hand. When you till the ground, it shall no longer yield its strength to you. A fugitive and a vagabond you shall be on the earth."

(Genesis 4:10-12)

You would think that being a fugitive and a vagabond, running from society for the rest of his life, would have been enough harshness bestowed upon Cain. What could hurt more than always being on the run, not being able to trust a single soul, living a life without ever being able to settle in one place? As unpleasant and difficult as his judgment was to be, it was nothing compared to the dagger to his heart felt when, from that day forward, the fruit of his labor would be cursed. The blessed yield of fruits and vegetables he was known for producing would only be a distant memory. Whatever he produced now in the field would not come close to the big and ripened food he had produced before his sin. The yield of his labor from this day forward would be a constant reminder that substituting presumption for faith was not worth it.

King Saul's Show of Presumption

Presumption was at the forefront of King Saul's demise. His potential to become a great king was limitless. It was his presumption that ultimately became his downfall. Never could anyone foresee the sad ending that would terminate his life, because he had everything Israel was looking for in their first king. His first grave mistake came when he believed that sacrificing without authority to do so would be overridden by the need. Surely there had to be exceptions to the rule, and the way he thought, this was one of those instances. In his tunnel vision, it would only be right to spiritually prepare his troops for war, even if that meant going beyond his jurisdiction to do so. At that time and place only priests and prophets could perform the sacrifice unto the Lord. Because the prophet Samuel was late in arriving for the sacrifice, Saul's impatience got the better of him and he jumped the gun. The prophet Samuel's anger over the incident caught him off guard because he was only trying to do a good thing by spiritually preparing his men for war. In his eyes, how in the world could a blood sacrifice given with the right spirit be rejected by God? His heart was not only in the right place, but he would also be performing a spiritual act. Saul's actions reminded me of a situation years ago when I was very new in the Lord and was the leader of our local youth group. Not knowing that our new mission work was exempt from offerings given to our district office, I took the responsibility of personally paying our youth group dues to our district officials. When called into the pastor's office to explain my actions, I was completely astounded by his anger. I thought taking the responsibility to help our small congregation would have been seen as something noble in the eyes of our pastor. But what I didn't know was that an arrangement had been made between our local church (actually a mission work) to be exempt from paying any monies owed to the sector or district. Without even knowing it, I had placed my pastor in an embarrassing position when he too had to explain why our youth group could comply with their financial responsibilities when the rest of the local church could not. I learned my first (and sad to say, not my last) lesson in presumption and the damage it could cause. Now then, we can return to Saul's dilemma.

An Unlawful Sacrifice

The answer, of course, comes when that same sacrifice was made unlawfully. In his limited understanding, Saul could not see that the Lord had everything covered and had already prepared Israel for ultimate victory. With this act of disobedience, he opened himself up to bad spirits, ones that would control and torment him for the rest of his life. Saul's reaction to the rejection was typical in that he shifted the blame for this mishap, putting it on his servant David, and for the rest of his miserable life his presumption haunted him to the grave. His final act of presumption: he overstepped his authority once again by taking the liberty to commit suicide.

...Therefore Saul took a sword and fell on it. And when his armorbearer saw that Saul was dead, he also fell on his

sword, and died with him. So Saul, his three sons, his
armorbearer, and all his men died together that same day.
(1 Samuel 31:4-6)

His presumption resulted not only in a cowardly suicide,
but was also responsible for the death of his three sons,
not to mention all of the soldiers who lost their lives in
battle that day. Presumption truly is a killer.

Presumption Disguised As Faith

One of Satan's most dastardly attempts to sway the
will of God in another direction is when he tries to
disguise presumption as faith. He is a master at
attempting to take the word of God out of context,
thereby confusing those he is dealing with to stray away
from the commandments of God. When Eve received
her orders from God, in actuality she had received them
secondhand from her husband, Adam. Like in most
cases when truth is communicated from one person to
another, there is a great possibility that clarity is lost in
the reception and the assignment does not get completed
the way it was originally ordered. Satan took advantage
of this by entering into the serpent so he could challenge
God's word. What the serpent had to say to Eve
appeared reasonable, but in actuality he knew without a
shadow of a doubt that his suggestion would be speaking
to her pride as well.

Then the serpent said to the woman, "You will not surely
die. For God knows that in the day you eat of it your eyes
will be opened, and you will be like God, knowing good
and evil."
(Genesis 3:4-5)

Her presumption had an opportunity to rear its ugly head when she pondered on the untrue promise that eating of the fruit would help both her and her husband to be like God. Who in their right mind could pass up an offer like that? What could possibly be bad about obtaining godlike characteristics? That day her presumption overrode her obedience, and without permission she took the liberty to eat of the fruit, which ended in a more harsh judgment that she could imagine. Her life was never to be the same, bearing children in painful labor and losing her place of authority in the garden to live in submission to Adam for the rest of her life. She had been created by God to rule the world side-by-side with her husband, Adam. He would demonstrate the more masculine attributes of God (power, strength, anointing etc.). With equal authority, Eve (Adam II-Genesis 3:20) would demonstrate to the world the softer side of God (love, joy, peace, etc.). Together they were to form the fullness of God on earth. Her presumption of what eating of the fruit could do for both her and her husband never came to pass. Of the two first creations of God, she was the one to suffer the greatest losses.

The Temptation of Jesus

It was those types of moral victories Satan used to garner up enough nerve to attempt fooling Jesus by using His own words against Him. He began by appealing to His hunger and bodily weakness after forty days of fasting in the wilderness.

And when He had fasted forty days and forty nights, afterward He was hungry. Now when the tempter came to

*Him, he said, "If You are the Son of God, command that
these stones become bread."*

(Matthew 4:2-3)

It was an appeal that he used successfully time and time
again with others who had proclaimed their allegiance to
God and only to Him. But when no one else was
looking, they cracked under the pressure and gave in.
Jesus would not take the bait, but rather used His word
to battle off the temptation.

*But He answered and said, "It is written, 'Man shall not
live by bread alone, but by every word that proceeds from
the mouth of God.'"*

(Matthew 4:4)

He ultimately refused to let presumption taint the use of
His gifting for personal gain. He knew that bread could
satisfy His physical needs, if needed, whereas the word
of God could accomplish the same task as well.

Appealing to God's nature was next on the list of
temptations, when again Satan used Scripture to trick
Jesus into doing something that would be ungodly. He
was trying to get the Lord to use the same character trait
that caused his fall from heaven; i.e., pride. This time
Satan would use God's word to bait Him. Look at the
results.

*... and said to Him, "If You are the Son of God, throw
Yourself down. For it is written: 'He shall give His angels
charge over you,' and, 'In their hands they shall bear you
up, lest you dash your foot against a stone."*

(Matthew 4:6)

If the Lord had complied with Satan's request, it would have surely drawn a big crowd, where at the same time it would ultimately show an unparalleled flair for the dramatic. God's response was clearly a demonstration of "who was in charge" when he responded:

> *Jesus said to him, "It is written again, 'You shall not tempt the Lord your God."*
>
> (Matthew 4:7)

Knowing that being rescued from a fall was not part of the plan to be received as the Savior of the world. The success of the Master would not be determined by falling down but by being lifted up.

> *And I, if I am lifted up from the earth, will draw all peoples to Myself*
>
> (John 12:32)

The final temptation Jesus had to endure was one that appealed to His purpose here on earth.

> *Again, the devil took Him up on an exceedingly high mountain, and showed Him all the kingdoms of the world and their glory. And he said to Him, "All these things I will give You if You will fall down and worship me.*
>
> (Matthew 4:8-9)

Satan offered him the world with one little catch: He must bow down and worship him. There would be no future obstacles, delays, or distractions in completing His earthly assignment. The road to victory could be one without shedding one drop of blood. I'm sure as Jesus mulled over the offer he came across one significant problem:…

>…*Without shedding of blood there is no remission.*
>
> (Hebrews 9:22)

Giving into Satan's demands would have demonstrated the ultimate act of presumption, taking the easy way out, one that the Lord never ever considered. Plodding around the road less traveled has always been God's way, why should He change now? After His last response to the devil, Satan fled in defeat once again.

Making a Paradigm Shift

Every successful Christian will have at one time or another to make a paradigm shift that will make his faith unmovable. What is a paradigm shift, per se? By definition, *it is a theory or a group of ideas about how something should be done, made, or thought about.*[9] The old adage (it's always been done this way, why change?) used for centuries does not hold water anymore. This shift God is requesting is the key that will unlock the door to the supernatural. Time is running out, with many souls yet to be saved. Our time left here on earth cannot be wasted by doing the same things over and over again, without any positive results. If we dedicate ourselves onto Him, He will be faithful to show us the way.

The apostle Peter wasn't quite ready for the great assignment the Lord was placing in his lap. The apostle Paul had not yet been converted, so the job to preach the Acts 2:38 message fell upon Peter by default. It was God's desire to use Peter to bring the salvation plan to the Gentile world regardless. His prejudices towards people not born as Hebrews was typical of the Jewish nation. The Jews always looked down upon anyone and everyone that was not born with the same blood as they. It wasn't so much that God chose to use a vision to speak to Peter on this occasion, because communicating through visions and dreams was commonplace. It was not much of a stretch for Peter to understand that God was truly speaking to him. It was more so the content of the vision that had Peter completely baffled. The instructions he received were abominable in that he was admonished to kill and eat unclean animals. For centuries this act was considered unlawful to the Hebrew nation, and breaking that law ultimately would be considered a blatant act of disobedience. How could God possibly contradict His word when it had been practiced that way for many, many years?

What Peter failed to realize was that the ceremonial law that he tried so desperately to keep without fail had been fulfilled when Jesus died on the cross. Without even having any knowledge of this paradigm shift, the temple curtain was torn immediately after Jesus died, which signified the dawning of a new era. For the first time in history, the salvation plan would take a change of direction never experienced before. Salvation would now be procured by repentance of the new believer, then being baptized in water in the name of Jesus, terminating this exercise with that infilling of the Holy Ghost by evidence of speaking in other tongues. (Acts 2:38) What would be even more difficult to comprehend and accept would be the fact that this salvation that was reserved exclusively for the Jews in the past would now be opened up to the entire Gentile world as well.

A vision from heaven was given to Peter to soften the blow of a Gentile servant who shortly would knock on Peter's door, requesting his presence at the home of his master. Even with sufficient warning, when the request was finally made, Peter's immediate reaction was that of disbelief and confusion. What was being asked of him was to disobey a custom that he and all Jews dedicated to their faith had obeyed for centuries. This request was not only preposterous, it was unlawful as well. The advantage Peter had in making this decision was the fact that he would not have to make it alone. On the day of Pentecost when he had received the gift of the Holy Ghost, the Spirit of God was not only given as part of the salvation plan, but its usefulness could extend out to our everyday lives as well. It would then prove to be a valuable asset in helping navigate us through the tough decisions coming our way. The end result: Peter preached a salvation message similar to the one on the day of Pentecost to an astounded group of Jews. Just as astonished were the group of Jews Peter had taken with him as a witness. Why? They were equally amazed when they got to see firsthand the Holy Ghost falling on unbelievers other than those of the Jewish faith.

When the initial shock wore off, their faith was increased to accept this new message and all that were listening to this Jewish man speak that day were saved. The Lord was able to make this happen even though Peter was not completely on board with this assignment. Although the Lord had gone out of His way to ensure that Peter would be a part of this great outpouring of God's Spirit, when the dust finally settled, Peter was still not totally convinced that what he had done was in actuality the right thing to do. History tells us that Peter's prejudice toward the Gentile nation continued until confronted by the apostle Paul and rebuked for his hypocrisy. (Galatians 2:11-14) That in and of itself made what happened on the day of Pentecost even more

93

mind-boggling and should be a lesson to us all even today. God will not wait until we have all our ducks in a row. He will use imperfect men and women to accomplish His will because the determining factor of being used by God is not perfection but availability. For one shining moment, Peter put his prejudice aside and allowed God to speak to people who were badly in need of salvation. It proved to be a moment that the entire world will never forget.

Why Churches Don't Grow

When it comes to dealing with presumption, it must be accepted that it is a major obstacle to the growth of the Church. Like tares being confused for wheat, presumption is a carnal man's faith. It lurks in the shadows, never making it clear enough to trust in. The reproach that tags along has far-reaching effects in that it allows people to discredit, disgrace, and blame God for not keeping His word. The disastrous outcome is not blamed on us, because as all could see we did our part in stepping out by faith (in reality it was presumption). If we do take that route in blaming ourselves for not having enough faith, we will always be in the doldrums without a clue as to why God is not answering our petitions. Nevertheless, because we were ill-informed, it is much easier to redirect our failures on God Himself than to accept responsibility for our presumptuous actions. What makes it even worse is that in the eyes of the unsaved, Jesus becomes another person in their lives who cannot come through with His promises. He, like all the others in their lives, will fall short of His promises. The opportunity of a lifetime for salvation in the lives of others is passed up because of a particular person's presumptuous actions that God never responded to.

Are your acts of faith truly initiated by God? When presumption is disguised as faith, it becomes one of the most diabolical plans, so well thought out that the blame for our failures is shifted from us to God Himself. Like a blind man, we grope around in darkness, not having a clue as to what God is demanding of us. We never seem to graduate from the "hit and miss" level of faith, and our spiritual growth is stunted. What is your life like? Is it a life of faith, dynamic and ever-growing? Or does presumption have you by the neck, squirming for your life, not knowing what will come next?

Our faith comes by hearing, not by presuming. A good work is only good when you are called by the spirit of God to accomplish it. It is then and only then that God has the responsibility to make the outcome of your faith a blessed one. If we don't let presumptuous sins have dominion over us, we can live our lives blameless and will be innocent of great transgressions.

CHAPTER 7

I NEVER SAW IT COMING

There is a way that seems right to a man, but its end is the way of death.

(Proverbs 14:12)

When presumption is in full bloom it will usher in disaster through the back door. The devastation caused is in many cases permanent and cannot be undone. The person awaiting his blessing will be blinded by something that came unexpectedly. The option for failure was never considered, because how could a godly work not succeed? The general consensus was that the faith demonstrated (not presumption) would bring the desired results and one could go on confidently to the next challenge. In its inception it seemed so right, how could anything possibly go wrong?

In another episode of Saul's disobedience, a closer look will provide proof that presumption, once again, was at the core of this mistake. When the Lord gave him another opportunity to redeem himself of his prior errors in judgment, sad to say presumption, not faith, got the better of him again. As commander-in-chief of Israel, Saul was not exempt in following God's laws and it was understood that he had to toe the line just as cautiously as those men and women under his rule. His disobedience was dealt with when Samuel, upon arriving to the camp, heard the bleating of sheep. When the prophet once again called Saul to the carpet, he again was caught off guard by Samuel's tongue lashing. In retracing his steps of what had just happened, he could not reconcile in his mind how sparing the best animals for sacrifice could be so wrong. When Samuel continued to survey Saul's disobedience, he found out that the disobedient king had spared the lives of the women and children as well. (It is highly possible that the Amalekite who later tried to take credit for Saul's murder was part of the remnant saved from death.) As the details of his sin continued to mount more evidence of his disobedience, in the end there was no place for him to hide. It was at this time he could have softened the blow of the judgment that would befall him. Yet, it was his failure to admit his wrong, and with a lie tried to cover up his mistake.

When Samuel rebuked Saul for his indiscretion, Saul never saw that coming. God's judgment hit him like a Mack truck blindsiding him into devastation and despair. He was never the same after the fact, so he found a scapegoat in the psalmist David, and from that day forward David would bear the brunt of the blame for all that was wrong in Israel.

Presumption Always Leads to Neglect

Presumption will always lead to neglect in one way or another. After suffering a stroke in 2013, one of the physical deficiencies that I was left with is what the doctors call "neglect." I can see out of both eyes, but it is the right eye that has been affected by the neglect. What it basically boils down to is I can see out of the right eye, but I am restricted in seeing only what is in front or to the left of me. My peripheral vision has been taken completely away and I am at a disadvantage when I am in public. When I am approached from my right side, because of the neglect, I don't see that person until they just about walk directly in front of me. It leads to a lot of scary moments, because it appears that people are always sneaking up on me and startling me. I have been instructed by the doctors, when out in public, to continuously be turning my head from left to right so that I would be able to see okay, and sneaking up on me would be kept to a minimum.

Although the turning of the head to scan all that is in front of me is an unnatural act, as far as the doctors are concerned, it is the only alternative to be able to see things like everyone else. They have said if I am going to have the ability to drive a vehicle again, something would have to be done to re-teach me the rules of the road using resources I already have but have never used. This concept is similar to what was done when the doctors decided to operate to repair the damage caused by my clogged arteries. In performing the quintuple bypass, they actually took the veins from both of my legs and transferred them to my heart. Five different bypasses were necessary to repair the damage caused by the clogged arteries that were at least 70 percent clogged, up to 100 percent. Just because what has been asked of me is unnatural compared to how I have survived in the past, does not mean that I can't use other resources to make ends meet. If anything, the lack of sight should by all means help me to compensate for this loss by using the other senses God created me with. Sharpening my skills in hearing, touching, feeling, and smell, if anything, will help me navigate through the loss of seeing to help me function properly as I move on in life. As I look back on my spiritual life, I realize that God has done the same thing as He has called me to a ministry of "signs and wonders." I have learned from experience that I cannot trust my eyesight and "walking by faith not by sight" has been a big part of that learning process. My greatest failures working in the Spirit have come when what I see in front of me does not reconcile with what God is telling me about the situation. It is a way that God would like to speak to all of us, if we were to only give Him that opportunity. When I have trusted Him, putting my own knowledge and experience to one side, it has created an atmosphere for God to move miraculously.

A Blind Man Wows Me

My loss of sight has reminded me of a great lesson I learned from a blind man I had the privilege of knowing when we taught together at a district junior camp. I will never forget this man of God because he left an indelible impression on me. The kids who had come to camp for seven days were between the ages of 12-14. They were a lively bunch, and at that age very rambunctious. Seeing that they were to be taught by a blind man had them licking at their chops. In their minds, they were going to have a field day with this helpless, overmatched handicapped man. You should've seen the shock on their faces when a student would try to sneak out of the room, only to be chastised and embarrassed by the blind teacher, who told him to sit down. When others tried to throw spit wads or throw any kind of trash, the teacher knew exactly who threw it and immediately put them in their place. After a couple of similar incidents, I was in awe over the reactions of those students and how the blind teacher had complete control over each and every one of them, even if he could not see them.

Presumption Leads to a Spiritual Neglect

When we are involved in spiritual matters, what appears right and correct is nothing more than a partial picture of the entire situation. What could ultimately destroy a life, relationship, career, etc., is hidden by the neglect and cannot be seen. A false sense of security overrides conventional wisdom until it's too late. The results then are disastrous and some irreparable.

The book of Proverbs, known for giving wise counsel, documents a situation where a young man is seduced by a harlot. His presumption of the situation resulted in a false sense of security that told him he could handle her advances without getting burned. If this young man would have been wise, he would have feared the situation and run from the evil. But because he was a fool, his self-confidence was his downfall. His presumption was strong enough to override his lack of experience. He never took into consideration the fact that he had never dealt with a woman with such persuasive powers, and yet he was very confident that he could hold his own on her turf. Whether it be man's pride or just his stupidity, it's amazing how a man will not desire to show any signs of weakness. On the other hand, the Scriptures say that a wise man knows when to run from danger and live to fight another day.

A wise man fears and departs from evil, but a fool rages and is self-confident.

(Proverbs 14:16)

Her flattering speech was unexpected and overwhelmed him till he yielded to her. The consequence of his error was more than what he had bargained for.

…He did not know it would cost his life.

(Proverbs 7:23)

In other words, **He never saw it coming!**

Joseph knew his limits in that he never put himself in a compromising position. His fear of God kept him from evil, even in the face of adversity. It allowed him to reject the sexual advances of his boss's wife. Even jail time could not convince him otherwise.

Trust in the Lord with all your heart, and lean not on your own understanding; In all your ways acknowledge Him, and He shall direct your paths.

(Proverbs 3:5-6)

If you choose to lean on your own understanding, it will always limit your options. Your neglect in spiritual matters will rule out the miraculous in your life. You'll never be able to see and embrace the great things God has prepared for you. Spiritually speaking, you will become that unloved redheaded stepchild, always a day late and a dollar short.

Avoiding Presumptuous Errors

Fighting through the layers of deceit will always be a major task. Satan's agenda is so well hidden that this reminds me of a theory I once heard about. It is called the theory of *six degrees of separation*,[10] and in the case of Satan deceiving us away from the perfect will of God, it would appear to apply. These layers run so deep that it is almost impossible to trace the origin of this dastardly plan. It is candy coated and appealing to the eye, and it goes down real smooth. The problem begins when deceit cannot be digested. Similar to what happens in a body physically when food is not digestible, it can cause sickness, and if not treated it can ultimately cause death. It is Satan's plan to fly so far under the radar that he will never be blamed for a lot of mayhem that enters into your life. When you finally get to the root, you are in so deep that making a rational decision is nearly impossible. When a decision is finally made, it is usually the wrong one. What appears too good to be true really is.

Nahash Threatens Israel

Israel found itself in a dilemma when it was caught in the desert in unfamiliar territory. The stress had grown to be unbearable, and to relieve the pressure they asked Samuel to let them be ruled by a king. God's perfect plan for direct fellowship was being rejected by His people. Having one man decide for them was less complicated and non-threatening. They wanted to serve the king that they physically could see and would make them similar to all the rest of the lands around them. They never felt that they could rally behind their leaders because they were not as majestic as those who were leading the other countries they had come across. The downside to Israel's request was that they were not to have a direct contact with God. They would find out quickly enough that this desire would not satisfy them as well. After the choice had been made to crown Saul the first King of Israel, many were not satisfied with God's choice, therefore their stress level did not subside. They began a never-ending journey for stress relief, one that could not be found.

Nahash the Ammonite had threatened Israel by setting up camp around them and their fear caused them to approach him with a peace offering. They wanted to secure a promise with him, with a covenant that would allow them to live peaceably under his rule without incident. Their fear played into his hand and the petition was simply to make a covenant with them, whatever it might be, and they in turn would serve him as their king. His counteroffer was somewhat unexpected and had caught them completely off guard. To Israel, much thought had to go into this decision, because he was asking for a lot more than what they were willing to give. What was the king's counteroffer?

> ... *"On this condition I will make a covenant with you, that I may put out all your right eyes, and bring reproach on all Israel."*
>
> (1 Samuel 11:2)

On the surface, although painful, it was doable and it far exceeded their only other option, which was to be killed by Nahash's army. To continue living, even under those painful conditions, would more than compensate for the loss of an eye.

The king's request of the right eye kind of perked up my curiosity to see if there was a particular reason why the right eye was chosen. Adam Clarke's commentary fills in the blanks with some background of 1 Samuel 11:2: *"He who opposes his shield to the enemy with his left hand, thereby hides his left eye, and looks at his enemy with his right eye; he therefore who plucks out that right eye makes men useless in war.*[11]

The ability to fight successfully was predicated on the use of their shields and without them they would be rendered helpless. The greatest impact of losing the right eye meant they would no longer be able to defend themselves expertly, and a warrior that cannot fight is an embarrassment to his country. What the king was counting on when he made this prospective deal was that this barbaric act would not only spell disaster for the Israeli army, but ultimately guarantee their utter submission to him. He could rest assured that there would be no problem from Israel because their ability to fight would have been taken away completely. Considering that in and of itself would mean the end of Israel as a powerhouse nation. They would always be at the mercy of people who did not know the one true God, and like it or not, deal with it.

Satan's Covert Use of Presumption

In trying to steer us off course by disrupting our vision, Satan's main objective is to cause the same in our lives. It is far easier to do than we think. We imagine that Satan spends all day long creating situations in our lives to help gross sin overpower us. What is even more evil and far more successful is the fact that the true definition of sin is nothing more than "missing the mark." He is most successful when he can get us to move either a little bit to the right or left to steer us off just enough to miss God and His perfect will. The sin of presumption is at the core of "missing the mark," and it doesn't take much to unravel the good God has tried to establish with His word.

Satan will go underground with his covert activities, using presumption as his primary weapon. We must be able to counter his attack with our most effective weapon, that being our faith. Faith must now become our weapon of choice if we are to defeat the enemy, rendering him helpless. Presumption cannot and will not hinder our destiny. Sad to say, our current definition of faith is the result of our limited vision. The full spectrum of faith must be adhered to if we are to go beyond our limited concept of faith, which has not brought much success to our lives up to this point.

Our current definition of faith is the result of our limited vision. Satan has successfully conned us into believing a definition of faith that has done us no good. Our concept of faith is so muddied and clouded by failure that we have no confidence "stepping out of the boat," per se, to do great things for God. The full spectrum of faith must be adhered to and set into motion because if not, we will never be effective in His kingdom.

I would like to share with you now a definition of faith that I was unaware of and most Christians today don't even realize exists. There is one foundational Scripture that has been used time and time again without the full revelation of its purpose.

So then faith comes by hearing, and hearing by the word of God.

(Romans 10:17)

Don't let the familiarity of the Scripture close your mind to what I am about to write. Most of you reading this at this moment will not pay too much attention, because from day one it has always been one of the most sacred, valued Scriptures in our arsenal. Yet it has been this one Scripture of faith that has not been completely understood. That lack of understanding has caused many a heartache because God did not respond to your so-called faith. This is what I wrote in my second book, "Unraveling the Mysteries of Faith." You will find this definition of faith completely different than what you're used to hearing and or reading. Don't dismiss it so quickly, let it sink in and let the Lord speak to you to see if this particular definition and its explanation will work for you.

We have been taught now for generations if that we hear the written word of God by whatever means, it will increase our faith. The fact of the matter is that it's both true and false. The key to understanding the Scripture in its entirety falls on the translation of the word, "word." Most of the time "word" is translated as "logos," and rightfully so. By definition, it translates as the written Word of God. The problem that we find in Romans 10:17 is that the Greek "word" used in this instance is "rhema." Rhema is translated as the "saying" word of God. Now then, there are times that the written Word can be rhema, but rhema doesn't necessarily have to be written for it to be the word of God. If we limit the definition of rhema to only the written Word of God, then we forfeit the Spirit of God speaking to us on a daily basis.

This is where most people miss it. In times of need, we have been taught to open up the Bible, find a Scripture that applies to our situation, and claim it by faith. Unless the Lord has specifically guided you to that particular Scripture and instructed you to live on it by faith, your efforts are nothing more than hit-or-miss. I have seen so many people use this method without success, that they have hopelessly given up on stepping out by faith completely.[12]

With both definitions functioning at the appropriate time, the full impact of a dynamic faith can be realized. It is no longer necessary to grope in the dark, blindly pursuing the presence of God without getting the answers you need. If we are willing to open our eyes without presumption, it will help us avoid ever saying, **I NEVER SAW IT COMING.**

CHAPTER 8

LET'S PLAY CHICKEN

... "I will never leave you nor forsake you." So we may boldly say: "the Lord is my helper; I will not fear. What can man do to me?"

(Hebrews 13:5-6)

The game of chicken is a game I'm sure that we all have played at one time or another. It is a game that has been played for generations and no one ever wants to be called "chicken." The game models two drivers, both headed for a single lane bridge from opposite directions. The first to swerve away yields the bridge to the other. If neither player swerves, the result is a costly deadlock in the middle of the bridge, or a potentially fatal head-on collision.[13]

The popularity of this odd-sounding game is one that has reached around the world and is displayed by young and old alike. The game in actuality has taken on a life of its own because the word "chicken" is used pretty much any time a challenge is requested. Whatever has caused a disagreement or a misunderstanding can usually be resolved by playing "chicken." The word has had such a negative connotation that no one in their right mind would ever allow someone else to take the liberty to say that to your face. You can almost say as they do in the South upon hearing this, "Them is fightin' words." Whoever is on the receiving end of those words will usually land up taking you outside to the backyard to show you that he's no chicken. It is amazing how Satan himself has used this particular tactic very successfully. It is part of his best con jobs, in that using fear negatively he has suckered many a man of God to lower himself to battle on Satan's turf. Once the fight is fought on his terms the outcome is never in doubt. When God is not fighting our battles for us, Satan will win every time. We all know that fear causes torment (1 John 4:18). As we continue to yield to it, it will work on us until we are completely broken. It is at that time that he will indirectly kill our blessing.

What Satan Does, God Can Do Better

What Satan can do, God can do better. He also uses fear to His advantage, but not in a satanic way. God's use of fear will yield our respect and will take us into a greater knowledge of Him. The difference between this fear that Satan uses so successfully and the fear God demonstrates to us in our lives, is the fact that God's fear is reverential (showing reverence) whereas Satan's use of fear will bring torment. Because the respect for God Satan has is so great, our reverence for the Master will cause our enemy to flee.

110

I will send my fear before you, I will cause confusion among all the people to whom you come and will make all your enemies turn their backs to you.

(Exodus 23:27)

If the word of God here in Exodus does not excite you and entirely motivate you to go on to bigger and better things in the Lord, you are certainly selling yourself short and not taking advantage of the power of His word. If we could truly understand the impact Scriptures such as these have, not only on our lives but on the enemy as well, we would be chomping at the bit to be used mightily of God. The fear that God projects unto Satan becomes more of a phobia than anything else. The Hebrew word for fear in this case is **krisisphobia**, meaning fear of judgment. Yes, Satan prances around as if he owns the entire world, but in reality everything that he does is motivated by fear. He knows how things will eventually end and how God has prepared a special place for him in eternity. It will be a place of utter torment.

Of course it is common knowledge that God's greatest use of fear against Satan was at Calvary. Satan's fear was so all-encompassing it cluttered and confused his thinking. Throughout the whole ordeal, Satan thought he was in control when in fact it was the Master's plan to give His life at Calvary for all of humanity. If he was as smart as he boasts to be, he would have heeded the wisdom of Pilate's wife when she tried to warn her husband of the severe error in judgment he was making. Pride got the better of our adversary because in the end he allowed Jesus to become the perfect sacrifice needed to bring salvation to a lost world. Killing Jesus would not end His ministry, it would define it. Remission of sins was not possible unless there was a shedding of blood, and one could not deny that the torture Christ endured both before (by whipping) and during (the crucifixion itself) was a bloodbath to be sure. With His blood being splattered in all directions, He gave His life for us.

One must come to the conclusion that playing "chicken" with God will always be a losing proposition. The cards will always be stacked in His favor, and in this case the house always wins. Because of Calvary, love is able to be so far-reaching that our past no longer haunts us. Our life in the present does not upset us, and as far as our future is concerned, it will not threaten us. Perfect love casts out fear (1 John 4:18) and now we are able to go on to bigger and greater things.

Elijah Vs Jezebel

In the aftermath of the great massacre we read of at Mt. Carmel in the first book of Kings, everything appeared to be set in order by Elijah to restore a backslidden Israel back to their God. They took the time to repent, getting back on track with the Lord, and Elijah in the interim became the hero of the hour. It did not take long for Jezebel, King Ahab's wife, to get wind of the humiliation of her priests before all of Israel. To add insult to injury, Elijah then took the bull by its horns and killed all of these false prophets. With that bit of news Jezebel became livid in her anger towards the man of God and threatened to kill him. Sad to say, her verbal rampage and empty threats caused Elijah to run because her words had gotten under his skin.

Then Jezebel sent a messenger to Elijah, saying, "so let the gods do to me, and more also, if I do not make your life as the life of one of them by tomorrow about this time."

(1 Kings 19:2)

Her written threat, although empty, made him come apart at the seams and run away like a little girl. Instead of standing up to her, his fear got the better of him and he decided to wait it out until the ruckus died down. She was certainly counting on Elijah forgetting who he was in God, and truth be told, he did. In God's eyes and in the eyes of all of Israel he was the godly man of valor. Israel and Judah were connected to God through this humble man's ministry. Because of his fear, his thoughts were so scrambled that doom was all he could think about.

If I were dealing with Elijah in this situation as God, my question to him would have been, "Elijah, what are you doing here? Can't you see that she is playing chicken and that she cannot back up her threats?"

Elijah Faced His Fears

When God restored his confidence, he got into the game without flinching. Elijah's anointing was evident when he did not lower himself to her level by responding with threats. With the spirit of God flowing all over him he responded with a promise instead.

And concerning Jezebel the Lord also spoke, saying the dog shall eat Jezebel by the wall of Jezreel.

(1 Kings 21:23)

It was the promise of Elijah that Jezebel mistook for a threat. Throughout her entire life she knew how to deal with even the most intimidating threats, and with experience had become a master negotiator. Her negotiations would never fail nevertheless; she was very effective in getting what she wanted. Of course, that meant bringing out the heavy artillery with no holds barred. She knew in the back of her mind that threats could always be challenged and negotiated. That was what playing "chicken" was all about. What she failed to realize was that our God doesn't play "chicken."

So shall my word be that goes forth from My mouth; It shall not return to Me void, but it shall accomplish what I please, and it shall prosper in the thing for which I sent it.
(Isaiah 55:11)

In hindsight, Jezebel never stood a chance. The problem for her was she never saw it coming.

A Day of Reckoning

Jezebel began to prepare herself as she always had by using all of her worldly ways of sprucing herself up. She brought out the sexy clothing, the expensive perfume with scents that would mesmerize, her exotic makeup from her homeland, and of course the latest hairstyle, always the attention-getter. She was literally, as they say, dressed to kill. She never came to the realization that she had met her match and then some in this man of God named Elijah. Jehu was then sent to deal with this wicked queen.

One final play of "chicken" was to be the order of the day. Defiant to the end, Jezebel mockingly reminded Jehu of his master, Zimri. Zimri had killed King Elah and overthrew his throne. His reign lasted seven days before sadly committing suicide. Jezebel then threatened

Jehu in the same manner, proclaiming that his authority was weak and his days were numbered, just like his master Zimri. Her playing "chicken" did not work. Her words had no effect on Jehu, so he commanded the men on the balcony with her to throw her out from a second story window. She was mortally wounded, and to make sure of her death, Jehu trampled over her with his horse, blood gushing out till there was no more life.

Playing "Chicken" In Milwaukee

In October 2013, as we were in the Milwaukee area preparing to minister to several churches there, I suffered a heart attack and stroke. For the next fifty-two days I would begin a period of suffering like I had never known before. It appeared to be open season on me and it was an experience similar to the one Job endured in the Old Testament.

And the Lord said to Satan, "behold, all that he has is in your power; only do not lay a hand on his person."

(Job 1:12)

Little did I know at that time that the weather was going to play a big factor in my test of faith.. That part of the country, as it turned out, had to endure one of the worst winters in recent memory. I remember when we finally escaped in December, it was right ahead of a storm that paralyzed Milwaukee for the next two weeks. As it was, the game began slowly but methodically. The Lord warned me ahead of time not to keep track of the days, because the longer I stood there Satan would be able to use that as a way of depressing me. With that warning, I usually kept the room darkened as much is possible. That way I would not know when days would begin and end.

The doctor's diagnosis was pretty plain and simple: I had suffered a stroke along with a heart attack. Upon hearing his words, they floored me in that I never realized that a heart attack was part of the problem I had when my vision went blurred. I had always imagined that having a heart attack would include a lot of chest pain and an endless amount of fear. Yet, to this day I could not tell you what it is to feel a heart attack because it was nothing like I had imagined. Because of the heart problem, it was decided to do further tests to see how badly damaged the heart was. It was at that time the doctors found five blockages that needed immediate attention. The clogging was major, sometimes up to 100% percent, the others were anywhere between 80 percent and 90 percent clogged as well. It was determined that I would need bypass surgery, which was to say the least a major operation. Before the doctors could repair the damaged heart, my body needed to regain strength, and I immediately began a program of physical therapy that would do the trick.

As the physical therapists worked on helping me get stronger, I started another type of therapy that would prove even more challenging. Because the stroke had affected my eyesight, it was in the part of the brain that also affects the memory. The speech therapy I was required to take was to help my memory by using techniques that would challenge me to the max. Of all the therapies that I was required to take (physical, speech, occupational), speech therapy was the one that worked more adversely than the others. I say that because the simple tasks that were part of the program were ones that in the beginning I was failing miserably.

Simple math problems and reasoning, not to mention the most difficult part of the therapy for me, the memorization really took its toll. The therapies were designed on an elementary level; in fact they were really games that were originally designed to help children. There were times of utter frustration, especially when I could not do simple math problems that in the past I could do in my sleep. For crying out loud, I was a math teacher in the past, teaching subjects anywhere from algebra to calculus, and in this instance I could not do simple math. Of course, the accuser was right by my side every step of the way, doing his best to rattle me, and to tell you the truth as time went on, it truly was working.

The game began to intensify, and it is amazing how such little things, insignificant things, were thrown at you all at once. They had such a great impact on both my thinking and my faith. The inconveniences grew bigger and more difficult to handle. For my entire stay in the hospital, my ability to sleep was taken away. It became common to toss and turn all night long, literally, and if I was lucky two hours of sleep would be the most I could get. My restlessness caused me to continuously look for a piece of furniture in the room that I could comfortably sleep on, whether lying down on my bed or sleeping sitting up on the various chairs that were in my room. This moving around from time to time all through the night had also affected my wife who, thank God, was with me for the entire hospital stay. I remember when I would wake her up in the wee hours of the morning to help me get out of the bed or chair that I had tried to sleep in, and never once did she complain. She was probably as tired as I was, yet with the patience of Job she was always there for me without complaining. Somehow at this time I was only averaging about two hours of sleep a night, yet I acquired bedsores that in and of themselves made a comfortable sleep impossible. If the soreness would have only been at night, it would have been much more bearable, but they bothered me throughout the day as well.

As I reminisce over all that I had to endure throughout my hospital stay, the aches, pains and inconveniences I had to put up with, if it would have been just one problem at a time I could have handled it. The greatest challenges I faced daily were dealing with a lot of little problems that appeared to be growing out of control. For example, because of the various shift changes throughout the day there were instructions and/or taking of medications that were either given in error or not given at all. I'm not sure how we were viewed by the staff when, after a while, we questioned everything, and rightfully so. If we had not taken the time to be so aware of what was going on it could have caused major problems.

The operation, they told me, was a complete success. However, in my mind I thought my physical condition was deteriorating instead of improving. I had assumed that after the operation my strength would return and I would be able to, with therapy, regain my strength as time went on. That was not the case, as I felt my physical condition was worsening instead of getting better. I tired more easily, which made it more difficult to function at my best in the various therapies. I realized then that I was not prepared for this mentally, and it came to me as a shock. My self-esteem continued to wane when I would get beat up emotionally in speech therapy, and it got to the point that I was dreading the time I would spend with my speech therapist. She was such a kind, mellow person, yet the nature of her job turned her, in my eyes, into the Wicked Witch of the West. I knew in the back of my mind that God had not forsaken me when my self-esteem was taking a big hit daily, nevertheless, it sure felt like it. There were times I felt I would suffer a nervous breakdown, and I was doing my best to trust God to take care of me. All the while, God was silent and He had removed His presence.

The intensity of the game grew more painful when I had adverse reactions to my medications. The painkillers I was initially given had caused dreams filled with anxiety. There were times I would wake up not knowing where I was and asking the most redundant questions over and over again. After the medication was taken away, the anxiety continued and I had never felt such spirits of fear that I felt during my hospital stay. If you have read any of my other books, you know that I have always admitted to a weakness that is heavily caused by fear. That being said, I had never felt spirits of fear as strongly as I had in Milwaukee. It was overwhelming that I could not think straight, my mind would race, causing my heart to beat in a way that felt like it would rip through my chest cavity, and I thought I was going to lose my mind. I could not believe it when the doctors had admitted that some of the medication I was taking caused the reactions that I was feeling. How in the world can a drug be sold that would cause such a negative side effect?

In trying to remedy the situation, they encouraged me to try breathing techniques. They even brought in a psychologist who would help me focus my thoughts on positive things. As I placed myself in the hands of these experts, again, nothing was successful in relieving my anxiety. I finally came to the conclusion that I was going to take this problem into my own hands and deal with it the one and only way that I had always dealt with my problems in the past. I told them that the next time an anxiety fit came over me, to please empty out the room and just let me pray. As simplistic as that sounds, it's the one and only way that I have always known to get me to a place of peace. The next time that an episode was coming up on me, I asked everybody to leave. At the top of my lungs I began to worship the name of the Lord. I know they could hear me out in the halls, and I really didn't care because I knew that my God was the only one who would be able to deliver me from this anxiety. The game of "chicken" had come to its apex and the devil was challenging me directly to see if I would back down and let him overtake my mind. There's only one way that I know how to pray effectively, and that's in the Spirit. I began speaking in other tongues and I did not care who was hearing me, all I knew was that I needed to touch God. Sometimes the battle would rage on for more than half an hour. In hindsight, there were times that I wasn't sure if God was going to come through. I kept on praying; calling on the name of the Lord, and every time the Lord would sweep into the room and rescue me.

After the first time I thought I had broken the curse, only to realize that Satan was not going to give up so easily. He continued to return, hoping to break my resistance, and as weak as I was at times I struggled through my prayer until my God had answered. I know that there were people on the medical staff who thought I was crazy, thinking how can a man as mild-mannered as he can get beside himself when he called upon his God? All I know is that God has never left me nor forsaken me, and even when I feel like it I still know that the word of God is true.

> *But know that the Lord has set apart for Himself him*
> *who is godly; the Lord will hear when I call to Him.*
>
> (Psalm 4:3)

I realize now, and in actuality have always known that the Lord has set me apart for Himself that He might be able to hear when I call on to Him. There's no greater confidence in this world than knowing a God who answers the cries of His children. I would have loved to write that the battle for my mind ceased immediately, but it did not happen that way. The battle continued for weeks and months, in actuality up until about a month after I left the hospital. When the Bible declares that we are to resist the devil and he shall flee, it's not a onetime resisting and voilà the matter is taken care of. There will be times that the battle is ongoing and your weariness will weigh heavy on your mind. But in those times you must remember His word.

> *...For He Himself has said, "I will never leave you nor*
> *forsake you." So we may boldly say: "The Lord is my*
> *helper; I will not fear. What can man do to me?"*
>
> (Hebrews 13:5-6)

The game of "chicken" can be played out in our lives over and over again, and yet if we will take this Scripture to heart, the end result will always be the same. Never is a long time, and that is an absolute promise that has victory written all over it. When we consider the far-reaching effects of His power and glory we can take on the boldness that this Scripture says we should have. When we determine in our hearts that the first portion of the Scripture is true, then we acquire the greatest helper we could ever obtain. With brimming confidence we can not only stand up against the enemy in fearless audacity, but we will also be able to ask this question in the Scripture above without having to ever back down. What can man do to me? Let's play "chicken" and find out!

CHAPTER 9

THE BIGGEST LOSER

To everything there is a season, a time for every purpose under heaven:... A time to gain, and a time to lose
                                            (Ecclesiastes 3:1, 6)

I was surfing the web a couple months back and I came across an article that I found amusing. There is a popular TV show called "The Biggest Loser," and there was a lot of attention given the young lady who had won the competition. According to the experts, she lost too much weight, way too soon, and instead of looking healthy, in their eyes, she had gone too far. Read an excerpt of the scandal that spread across the nation:

From the looks of coaches Jillian Michaels and Bob Harper's face, they may have been thinking what just about everyone on Twitter and Facebook has been posting: *The Biggest Loser* winner Rachel Frederickson is too thin. Rachel, 23, went from 260 pounds to 105 pounds (a total of 155 pounds shed), losing 60 percent of her body weight, thus making her $250,000 richer.upon seeing her, Jillian mouthed, "Oh my God!" Rachel's dramatic transformation caused quite the weight debate among viewers of the NBC reality show, with many using the hashtag #anorexia when referring to her weight loss.[14]

Whether she had lost too much weight or not is truly debatable. If medical doctors have given her a clean bill of health, then "losing too much weight" is in the eye of the beholder. It boggles my mind when I read about success stories that are highly criticized. The great adjustments that had to be made to get to the point where they are at today were not easy, if nearly impossible. There will always be a negative spin on people who do what others feel is impossible. Whether it be pure jealousy or just another way to rationalize why they themselves cannot do the same, the criticism goes on. In this case, losing so much weight put her in the category of a "loser." Of course, the connotation of that particular word is far from positive. No one in their right mind, in this society, would joyfully accept that label, because with it comes a lot of grief.

People who are considered "losers" in our society are the bottom feeders no one wants to become. A loser, in many respects, is a quitter, one without enough heart to finish anything they have started. They are negative in their thinking and there always appears to be a rain-filled cloud just above their head waiting to burst with a shower that will put a damper on anything and everything they will try to accomplish. The word has such far-reaching effects in one's life that even considering a happy ending to a problem really becomes a stretch.

A loser might as well be lazy because a lazy person has the same morbid results. A lazy person will never win because a winner is never lazy.

> *Go to the ant, you sluggard! Consider her ways and be wise, which, having no captain, overseer or ruler, provides her supplies in the summer, and gathers her food in the harvest. How long will you slumber, O sluggard? When will you rise from your sleep?*
>
> (Proverbs 6:6-9)

In a country (United States) that rewards laziness (welfare) there is a constant battle to ignore the Scriptures regarding the hard-working ant. Wisdom would be easily available if we would just consider her ways. No one tells her what to do or how to do it, somehow in her mind she will be able to figure it out. You would think that with the help of the Spirit of God we would be motivated to work hard to gain the success we are all looking for. But, sad to say, the easy road is chosen more times than not, and our "loser" label hangs from our neck like an albatross.

Spiritual Losers

As bleak a picture as I have painted of the so-called "losers" in our lives, the Scriptures encourage us to go that route and become spiritual "losers." Losers not like those we find in the world today, but the type of loser God can use for His honor and glory. Is there such a thing? Although our society teaches us that winning is everything and perhaps the only thing, in reality we go to extremes to avoid losing. Even if it is encouraged in the kingdom of God, our so-called common sense won't allow us to cross that line. Why? Because we handle losing so miserably. In our way of thinking, the time for losing is a time for whining, complaining, and making excuses. We will do anything and everything in our power to distance ourselves from being called a "loser."

This mentality of avoiding that label has caused paranoia, believing that a "loser" is nothing more than a modern day leper. The Old Testament leper was treated like a second class citizen with no rights at all. Because his disease was incurable it automatically made him an outcast in society, with a negative outlook like few others. Lepers were completely ostracized and were not able to function normally with family and friends. They lived in isolated neighborhoods far away from those who could easily catch the dreaded disease that could possibly lead to a premature death. Because of their isolation they were restricted to living and fellowshipping only with their kind. That was the only family they would ever know.

A Modern Day Leper

Years ago while I was pastoring, one of the members of our congregation at that time was a former leper. I say former because the Lord actually healed him of the disease. He is a typical big, strong, gregarious, Samoan man, and the only telltale sign that he had been stricken with that death sentence was a slight closing of his right eye. Other than that, you would have thought that his growing up here in the United States was normal and carefree. I remember him telling me that as a small child growing up in Hawaii, his life was pure bliss. With beautiful beaches and tropical rain forests, Hawaii truly was for him heaven on earth. One day as the family traveled to the other side of the island for a picnic, they came to an area that he was unfamiliar with. He was then introduced to some men of God, and in turn left his family to go play on the beach. When he returned after frolicking in the water, his parents were nowhere to be found. He searched high and low for them but never did they appear. It was then that those in charge of the leper colony informed him that the island would be his new home. Because he was stricken with a contagious disease, he could no longer live in civilization as he had known it. The news of his new fate nearly crushed him. I remember him recounting to me the many lonely nights spent on that beautiful island, crying himself to sleep. It wasn't until the Lord had actually healed him miraculously that he had been released from both his death sentence and his prison sentence. He was a "loser" of another kind, yet he was ostracized in a different way.

Thank God, the Lord sees losing in a different light. It is the difference between night and day because in His eyes losing will bring with it an eternal life in glory. We must come to the realization that eternal life with Jesus is for winners, not losers. Truth be told, losing our lives for His sake is the best thing that could ever happen to us. If that is really true, then why do we fight so hard to avoid it? I can tell you exactly why. Losing has always included persecution (causing to suffer for beliefs), which then leads to tribulation. It is this tribulation (a distress coming from persecution) that brings to a life bitter grief.

Yes, and all who desire to live godly in Christ Jesus will suffer persecution.

(2 Timothy 3:12)

You would think that giving your life to the Lord would bring back complete peace and harmony in your life. As much as that is true, with those characteristics being an important part of your life, being persecuted will be a telltale mark that you are living a godly life as the Scriptures implore us to do. If there is no persecution from the outside world, then there is something wrong in your service to Him and your growth and maturity will be stopped in its tracks. I understand this warning of what living for God is all about is somewhat painful and bleak, but understand that living a blessed life in God means that persecution cannot be avoided.

When Persecution Produces Tribulation

The Lord is not a sadist in any way, but understand that allowing persecution to shape our lives in Him has its merits. What good could possibly come from tribulation?

> ... *But we glory in tribulations also: knowing that tribulation works patience...*
>
> (Romans 5:3 KJV)

The Scriptures also tell us that in our patience we possess our soul (Luke 21:19) and it behooves us to build our patience through our suffering. It is with that mindset that we can overcome even the most severe tribulation, because Scripture admonishes us that Christ has overcome the world and its tribulation with an overwhelming success.

*These things I have spoken to you, that in Me you may
have peace. In the world you will have tribulation; but be
of good cheer, I have overcome the world.*

(John 16:33)

It is good to know that even in the most difficult of
times, peace can reign in our hearts. It is with that
knowledge that the phrase "peace in the midst of the
storm" can be understood and embraced. People in this
life who do not know Jesus Christ as their personal
savior will never be able to comprehend the Lord's
words, because in their eyes tribulation becomes nothing
more than a necessary evil. They are willing to bear the
burden of this troublesome time, not because it is
beneficial to their Christian walk, but because in their
eyes, there is no way around it. They take the attitude
that they must just grin and bear it, if that at all, and will
continue their lives never really taking full benefit of this
trying time.

Learning Through Tribulation

Job's training in the kingdom of God came through
severe tribulation. The humility that he lacked could
never be cultivated to perfection until he was asked to
endure an enormously painful period of suffering. The
prosperity that he used as his emblem of success could
never provide the experience that humility would be able
to accomplish. The goodness of the Lord only spoiled
him, giving him an unrealistic view of God. He viewed
God as the ultimate provider, a spiritual genie if you will,
and one that would always be there to satisfy his every
whim. What exactly happens in a person's life when what
is asked for is constantly given without any type of
struggle? What will it show to the world as far as his

personality and character goes? Finally, what valuable lessons of life are never learned because adverse conditions were never given the opportunity to strengthen that character? Anyone who has not had the opportunity of being humbled in God's school of humility will lack the necessary wisdom to be a success in the things of the Lord. That is how I pictured Job before his earth-shattering experience with suffering. He was proud and impatient, and his character reeked with intolerance, truly in need of an attitude adjustment.

When Job decided to make daily prayers unto the Lord for the health and welfare of his children, in reality he was doing them a disservice. It wasn't so much that God would not hear his petitions before Him, but it was Job's attitude that had fallen short. How so? Job took the time to get on his knees daily to secure health and safety for his entire family. What could be possibly wrong with that? Doesn't every dedicated Christian do the same? Yes and no. It wasn't his actual prayers that were necessarily wrong, but the fact that there is no recorded evidence that he taught those children how to pray themselves. It was so much easier for him to take his gift of intercession to the throne of God than to teach those same principles of prayer to his children. His diligence in his prayer closet would never be passed on to the next generation. It was enough for Job to have a personal relationship with his God, rather than to struggle with his kids who perhaps would not have the same desire to touch God as did their father. Job was neglecting one of the greatest commandments written by the wisest man who ever lived:

Train up a child in the way he should go: and when he is old, he will not depart from it.

(Proverbs 22:6)

What Job's Prayers Were Really Saying

When Job decided to take on the responsibility of touching God's throne in behalf of his children without teaching them to have a personal life with that same God, he was indirectly disobeying one of the greatest commandments the Lord has given to us as parents (Proverbs 22:6). For future generations to continue in the ways of the Lord, our ways of belief must be directly passed on to our children by us, the parents. It is not the responsibility of the pastor or the Sunday school teacher, per se, but God has chosen a more direct way for children to grasp His word. Never in his wildest imaginations did he believe that his resolve would be challenged by what came next. He assumed that by covering all the bases with his intercessory prayer it would be sufficient to pass on to his children the great blessings God had bestowed upon him.

His diligence in prayer, constantly petitioning God in behalf of his children, was actually demonstrating his impatience to do the right thing. That doesn't sound right because the Scriptures describe Job as a perfect man. If what he was doing and how he was praying was off kilter, then the Scriptures describing him are false. We know that the Bible does not lie and also does not contradict itself, so we must dig somewhat more deeply to reconcile the differences.

And the Lord said unto Satan, Hast thou considered my servant Job, that there is none like him in the earth, a perfect and an upright man, one that feareth God, and escheweth evil?

(Job 1:8 KJV)

The Hebrew word for perfect is (**taam**), which translates into the word pious.[15] That being said, a more meaningful definition for perfect would be his reverence for God, which was impeccable. Job's dealing with people, on the other hand, left something to be desired. In my lifetime I have come across quite a few perfectionists. Although they would appear to be great achievers, on the other hand their patience is spent quite easily. They fly off the handle at the drop of a hat when an imperfection is brought to their attention. They will almost foam at the mouth, chomping at the bit when a project is not completed in a timely fashion, and whoever is responsible for that failure will hear about it loud and clear. No one can say anything to them because they know it all. As much as they are admired in most circles because of their ability to get things done, people just put up with them because there is no reasoning with a perfectionist. The motto, "it's either my way or the highway" is their mantra, one that they hold closely to their hearts. That, my friend, is a snapshot of what Job portrayed to the rest of the world, and consequently God had to deal with him to make him a better person.

A Sidebar

Let me take a side bar here for a moment and include something I feel is important for the church of today to hear. We as a Church have become somewhat pious in our dealings with others. I know that when it comes to our worship unto God we are almost impeccable with that personal offering given to the Lord. But there is an underlying reason why our churches are not growing at the rate God promised us in His word. Our people skills are lacking big time, and it's not so much that people are rejecting God as we share the good news with them; in reality, they are rejecting us. We need to lose some things; i.e., our inhibitions, insecurities, and the desire to hoard all of God's blessings. In God's economy that will ultimately make us the winners God had projected us to be.

I could definitely identify with this man of God. In the eyes of others he was beyond reproach, not to mention the great wealth he had accumulated. Read his resume if you will, because compared to other people in his life time his blessings were far and above anyone on the earth, ones that garnered the utmost respect.

And seven sons and three daughters were born to him. Also, his possessions were seven thousand sheep, three thousand camels, five hundred yoke of oxen, five hundred female donkeys, and a very large household, so that this man was the greatest of all the people of the East.

(Job 1:2-3)

My identifying with Job had nothing to do with reputation or wealth. I have never worn expensive clothes nor driven a fancy car. For most of my life the home or apartment we lived in was rented, not bought. Our vacations were not extravagant in that most of the time while ministering we stayed in the area afterward to take our rest. When I mentioned that I could identify with this Old Testament patriarch, I meant to say we both have had similar relationships with our God. Prayer for the most part has always been a delight, not a chore. I'm sure that in one of my books in the past I have mentioned what I am about to write, but it bears repeating. Every time I enter into my room to be alone with God, I always take the opportunity to tell Him that what I am doing as far as prayer is concerned will be more important to His kingdom than anything else I will accomplish in ministry for Him.

I am now months away from my 60th birthday (what an old buzzard I have become), and as I look back on my life and what has transpired, the label of suffering could be attached to my life without it being a stretch. Because God has undoubtedly known from the outset that I would keep my promise to share with anyone and everyone willing to listen of the adversity I have faced in my life, it would appear that I have suffered more than most children of God. I do not write this to patronize anyone reading this book, nevertheless my willingness to share in what has happened to me and how God has always brought me out successfully, made me a perfect candidate to spend a lot of time in His "school of suffering."

What I Have Learned in God

What have I gleaned from these gut-wrenching experiences? I have learned that every promise of protection, deliverance, and well-being found in Scripture have rung true in my life at the most difficult of times. Every time the Lord delivered me from harm's way or physical disease, the result has been to receive a greater revelation of the grandeur of my God.

I will praise the name of God with a song, and will magnify Him with thanksgiving.

(Psalm 69:30)

How could I possibly magnify the Lord's greatness and majesty, when in fact without my praise they are still endless? What that praise actually does for me and anyone else willing to do so, is to magnify the greatness of our Lord in our eyes personally. Literally, you can't make God any bigger in His attributes than He already is, except in your own eyes. That is how our appreciation for Him continues to expand daily and grows deeper in our hearts.

The Biggest Loser Ever

If there was an Academy award for the "biggest loser" in real life, that award would certainly go to the Lord Jesus Christ. As blasphemous as that might sound, losing His life was the only way the Lord could accomplish His goal of bringing salvation to a lost world. The punishment meted out when a man was crucified was a punishment reserved for the "biggest losers" of society. Yet the Lord was willing to take on that role and ridicule that ensued to buy the salvation of an entire world with the shedding of His precious blood. This punishment of death was considered a curse in those times.

Christ has redeemed us from the curse of the law, having become a curse for us (for it is written, "Cursed is everyone who hangs on a tree")

(Galatians 3:13)

Losing His life was not as easy as everyone makes it out to be. His agony at Gethsemane is well chronicled, and just the fact that His sweat began to fall like droplets of blood goes to show that the anxiety pressed upon Him was one that few have ever experienced. He even went to the extreme to plead for another way of dying if it were at all possible. Ultimately He knew that to save a life, another one had to be lost so He took on the role of a sacrificial lamb and cried out,... *"Nevertheless not my will, but thine, be done."* (Luke 22:42)

As I close out this chapter on "losers," it is only right to bring to light three ways of losing out with God and how to avoid them:

1. Loving your life (more than God) -- *He who loves his life will lose it, and he who hates his life in this world will keep it for eternal life.* (John 12:25) *Whoever therefore wants to be a friend of the world makes himself an enemy of God.* (James 4:4)

2. Saving your life (holding back) -- *For whoever desires to save his life will lose it, but whoever loses his life for My sake and the gospel's will save it.* (Mark 8:35)

3. Finding your old life (worst option) -- *As a dog returns to his vomit, so a fool returns to his folly.* (Proverbs 26:11)

Understanding that losing can be beneficial in the kingdom of God doesn't necessarily label your entire life as a "loser." It has been ordained of God at certain times of our lives that losing will bless us.

> *A time to get, and a time to lose; a time to keep, and a time to cast away;*
>
> (Ecclesiastes 3:6)

As long as it is in the framework of God's will, you really have nothing to lose and everything to gain.

CHAPTER 10

OUT FROM THE WILDERNESS

Then Jesus was led up by the Spirit into the wilderness to be tempted by the devil. And when He had fasted forty days and forty nights, afterward He was hungry.

(Matthew 4:1-2)

Then the devil left Him, and behold, angels came and ministered to Him.

(Matthew 4:11)

The wilderness described in the Bible played an important part in the spiritual growth of the people of God. Examine with me the details of what it meant to be in a "wilderness" situation.

The general term "wilderness" may sound like it refers only to desolate or desert areas, but in the context of <u>Palestine</u> it has wider <u>connotations</u>. Wilderness isn't just a *type of place, it's also a concept when it comes to biblical texts. The Hebrew word used for wilderness, **midbar**, doesn't just mean "a desolate and deserted place," it also means "that which is beyond." Typically, it means "beyond" organized settlements, the control of the government, and traditional civilized norms. Usually the biblical references to Wilderness are negative: it's a place of thirst, hunger, deprivation of all sorts, windswept, haunted, etc. ...Quite often prophets wandered in the wilderness to be "tested" or "tempted," thus making the wilderness a place of spiritual renewal. Surviving in the wilderness demonstrated that one was able to overcome physical and psychological dangers — not just because one was cut off from ready sources of food or water, but also from their community. Whenever the Bible references a wilderness, readers should look beyond the mere physical manifestation and consider the wider ramifications of what it might mean.[16]*

There is another definition of wilderness that must be paid close attention to. Webster approaches it from a different angle, but needless to say it is just as important to include it in our discussion to be able to get a full spectrum of what a wilderness experience includes:

(1): a tract or region uncultivated and uninhabited by human beings (2): an area essentially undisturbed by human activity together with its naturally developed life community[17]

With both definitions carrying equal weight, the discussion can continue as to how wilderness experiences affected and continue to affect a child of God.

The Importance of Both Definitions

Both definitions certainly apply to the Christian life in that at times our wilderness experiences can be completely dry, or on the other hand, our spiritual wilderness can include such thick foliage that it is extremely difficult to make your way through it. There is not a soul on this earth that delights in their wilderness experiences because their survival techniques are challenged to the max. From one extreme to the other, the wilderness exposes weaknesses and/or our patience. There are no shortcuts in the wilderness and only through a maximum effort (including blood, sweat, and tears) can we safely exit this experience.

Our perspective of the spiritual wilderness experiences must do an about-face in that they are allowed into our lives, not to destroy us, but rather strengthen our resolve. It is a staple requirement in our class of Spiritual Growth 101. If you truly want to be used by God, you have got to get it into your head the only way to victory is through the wilderness. If you don't believe me, take a look at the following examples that are sprinkled throughout the entire Bible. Every man or woman mentioned here had a wilderness experience, one which defined them, not destroyed them:

Moses came out of the wilderness to part the Red Sea. Joshua came out of the wilderness to command the sun to stand still. When little David came out of the wilderness, he came out to kill Goliath the giant. Elijah's coming out party from the wilderness allowed him to call down fire from heaven. The apostle Paul got into the act by turning the world upside down when he came out of the wilderness. How could we forget the three Hebrew boys who would not burn in the furnace because they chose to stand for God in the wilderness? Queen Esther was able to save a nation by entering the wilderness of fasting and prayer and receiving a word of knowledge that sealed the deal. Finally, the apostle Peter preached the greatest message of salvation on the day of Pentecost right after picking himself up out of the wilderness to preach the Acts 2:38 message.

I know from experience that when scriptural references are mentioned to inspire us to greater heights in our spiritual walk with God, many times they intimidate us more than help. What we take from these bigger than life stories is that in our lifetime, in our culture, we could never live up to the spectacular feats done by these super servants of God. That being said, if any of the aforementioned vessels of God were to sit down with us and share the intimate details as to how their victories came about, we would be able to understand that they were a lot more like us than what we think. I believe I can move on to the next section of wilderness experiences without sounding like I have overly exaggerated the details. Whereas at one time, testimonies like the one I will write about were ones that I honestly felt were beyond my reach. When you read this first testimony you will understand why.

An Experience I Will Never Forget

It was 1974, two years removed from my decision to leave my football career to serve the Lord. As we made our way to our annual youth convention in Phoenix, Arizona, my heart was divided as to being away from home when USC was to play their bitter rival, Notre Dame, in Los Angeles. I was still feeling the aftereffects of not accepting my full ride scholarship to the University of Southern California and I really needed an emotional lift. It was at about the same time as the game was to start we were scheduled to attend a youth banquet. A special speaker was invited, Donald Deck was his name and he was the youth president for the UPCI. The testimony he gave that day, more so than an actual preaching message, is one I will never forget even forty years later because of the impact it had on my spiritual life. The details may be a little fuzzy and I hope I do this testimony justice because it was the first testimony that introduced me to the ministry of angels. I will use the documented information to describe the events of that day and then use my memory to describe the aftermath.

Forty-seven years ago, ex-Marine Charles Whitman walked to the top of the Austin's University of Texas' 307-foot clock tower and shot at students and Austinites for over 90 minutes with an array of firearms, all told killing 15 people and wounding 32 during his August 1, 1966 killing spree. A trained Marine sniper, he shot most of his victims near the heart. Whitman killed his mother and wife in the hours before he began shooting from his perch in the observation deck of the 27-story clock tower, just before noon on August 1, 1966. He wanted to spare them the shame of living with his deeds. During his terrorizing three-hour tantrum, he shot a pregnant woman, Claire Wilson, killing her unborn child with a gunshot to the head while still in the womb. Wilson survived but would not be able to have any more children. The child was the sixteenth Whitman victim, yet sometimes the baby is not listed in the final tally of the dead. Three decades later a seventeenth death would be attributed to Whitman when in November 2001 David Gunby died of injuries he suffered when he was shot that day. He had been shot in the lower back, destroying his kidney, leading to a kidney transplant and a life of dialysis treatments. Following more than an hour of mayhem on the UT campus Whitman was so terrifyingly accurate with his high-powered rifle that he shot people as far as 500 yards away. McCoy and a small group of others made their way to an observation deck atop the 28-story tower. McCoy fired twice from his 12-gauge shotgun, shooting Whitman in the face.[18]

As the bullets began to fly on that fateful day, the precision of this sharpshooter was impeccable. He randomly chose his victims, and with one of those bullets hit a young man by the name of Adrian Littlefield. A student at the time, he was also a young, aspiring evangelist. His future was bright as he had dedicated himself to the Lord and it showed in the revivals he preached. Receiving the Holy Ghost was a common fixture to this young man's ministry, and surely his best years were ahead of him. Because Whitman was such an expert marksman one shot was usually a kill shot. When this rifle was aimed at Littlefield, the bullet did not instantly kill him like most of the others, but the wounds would prove to be mortal if he did not arrive at the hospital in time. In hearing the news reports that were being broadcast, his father made a last ditch effort to get to the university. Not knowing for sure whether his son had been involved in the shooting or not, he wasn't going to take anything for granted and arrived as soon as he could. Somehow through the confusion, Mr. Littlefield found his son amongst the wounded. Adrian was then transported to a nearby hospital, but as he rode in the ambulance the loss of blood was causing him to lose consciousness. The paramedic told the father adamantly that if his son were to fall asleep there was a good chance he would die. He had to do anything and everything in his power to make sure that he was awake when the ambulance drove into the emergency section of the hospital. The weakness felt by Adrian was such that he was drifting away, so keeping his eyes open was nearly impossible. When he did not respond to his father's voice to stay awake, his dad began to shake him, hoping that that would do the trick. When Adrian would not respond to the shaking, his father went a step further and began to punch his son in the face. As much as it hurt this dad to take such an extreme course of action, it was necessary to keep him alive.

Arriving At a Hospital in Chaos

When they finally arrived at the hospital, again it was a chaotic mess. As much as Mr. Littlefield tried to exude the utmost patience, in reality Adrian was dying. Mr. Littlefield was beside himself and started to lift his voice in a matter of desperation. "You've got to do something for my son," he shrieked. "He has a call of God on his life and he cannot die." With much determination, he finally convinced a doctor to work on his son immediately. Long story short, the life of Adrian Littlefield was saved. The diagnosis for his recovery was bleak in that the doctors said that his paralysis would never allow him to walk again. The Littlefields never believed the doctors' report and consequently never lost hope. A short time later when Adrian was released from the hospital, he did so walking on his own two feet. He was not completely healed, for he would tire easily, and considering the condition of his health he would have to find something else in the kingdom of God other than evangelizing throughout the country because it would be too taxing on his body.

Although he lived to fight another day, that fight would not include the ministering of the gospel as he had known it before. He would have to adjust to this way of thinking and come to the realization that this new wilderness experience would change his life forever. He continued to minister here and there, and when opportunities arose to pastor a church he politely refused. He did not want anyone to feel sorry for him and patronize him just because of a debilitating handicap. These offers to pastor various churches continued until one day he accepted an offer.

Pastoring Under Adverse Conditions

Even putting all of the physical effort he could muster, it was only good enough to get him to the pulpit once a week on Sunday. That one day of ministering would exhaust him so much so that it would take approximately two to three days for him to recover. It was with this kind of effort that revival broke out in that little church. It quickly was filled and the congregation immediately began to work on securing a more ample building for their ministry. When the funds were available to make that move, there was a special inauguration service programmed. It was at this particular service that Donald Deck, the international youth president at that time, attended this special celebration. I remember him (Deck) saying this in recounting the story when he entered into that packed out church, knowing that the pastor himself could barely speak once a week and only for fifteen minutes at that. How in the world did revival breakout?

He surveyed the crowd from the platform, again wondering what was the secret of this handicapped man that brought such great growth to this church? It was then that the Lord opened his spiritual eyes and he understood why. As he gazed into the congregation from side to side, front to back, he saw angels standing at attention, waiting for their command to minister revival to those hungry folks. He had never seen anything like it, and was so amazed by God's show of power he realized that there is a dynamic released in the Spirit when one comes out of the wilderness. His mind immediately went to the portion of Scripture when Jesus Himself came out of a similar situation.

Then the devil left Him, and behold, angels came and ministered to Him.

(Matthew 4:11)

One of the greatest examples Jesus left for us is found in this portion of Scripture. The King of kings and Lord of lords, the creator of the universe, humbled Himself for forty days of prayer and fasting. I believe what drove Jesus to the wilderness for this time of spiritual dedication wasn't so much so that He needed it. I honestly believe He humbled Himself to set a precedent for us to follow in our spiritual lives so we too could be as successful as He would coming out of the wilderness.

My Understanding of Angels Changed

It has been almost forty years since my understanding of the ministry of angels changed. They have been commissioned to help us in whatever ways possible with their personal ministering to us, the

145

children of God. Some might be asking at this point in time if the testimony I have given is actually a normal occurrence or is it just an every once in a while kind of thing. Well, I can only recount the things that I have seen and heard, so I will finish this chapter with a testimony that happened to me a couple of years ago.

When I was ministering in California a few years back, a special move of God shook the entire congregation from the front to the back. It was the type of move that God makes sovereignly every once in a while without notice. It had nothing to do with our worship that day, neither had the congregation overly prepared itself in extended prayer and fasting, it was just God showing off because He wanted to. As the intensity of the service continued to grow, there was a portion where there was dancing at the altar. One young man in particular was in a spiritual tizzy when the Spirit of God slew him in the Spirit. After this monstrous demonstration of God's power subsided and it was time to deliver the word, the young man stayed flat on his back at the altar for the rest of the service's duration. Several hours later, when everything calmed down and the service was dismissed, the young man came up to me and said something I will never forget.

He said, "Brother Pantages, while I was slain in the Spirit although my eyes were closed during the entire time, the Lord took the opportunity to show me what was going on in the spirit realm. I saw a giant angel behind you trying to encourage us to release our faith to go on to bigger and better things. There was such a distressed look on his face because we as the people of God could not accept the offer of greater success in our lives to be a daily occurrence. After a period of time trying to convince us of that fact, he finally gave up and left."

I have never forgotten what that young man told me that day about his experience with God. It saddened me to think we forever shun our responsibility of allowing God to take us through our wilderness experiences. We would rather play it safe like the soldiers of Israel when the giant Goliath was challenging their existence and faith. It is easier not to rock the boat for fear of falling, or often drowning, but somebody has to step up and take God at His word. Are you willing to allow ministering angels into your life as you make it through your wilderness experiences? All I can say is that if you do make that choice, you will never be the same again.

EPILOGUE

I had the opportunity of having my friend Jeffrey Arnold look over this manuscript before it was sent to print. As we began to discuss the intricacies of my writings I was set aback by his observations. It was in his opinion that I had not clearly explained the hows and whys of going deeper in our relationship with the Lord. It appeared to me that he was looking for a manual that would step-by-step lead him into a deeper relationship with God. As I began to seek the Lord for an explanation, this is what God told me:

"The deep things of God cannot be passed along from one person to another by teaching or observation. They must be received from God personally on a one to one basis, realizing that each experience in God will be different. As far as God is concerned the outcome or the result may be the same for those that are searching for a deeper relationship with Him. Nevertheless, the journey will always be distinctive and unique. Trust in God has to be considered the most valuable attribute a child of God has to place in His hands so that the perfect will of God may be attained. The proverbial light at the end of the tunnel will not be discovered and seen at a first glance. In His time and with our patience, the perfect will of God will unfold right before our own eyes. It is in the audience of the King that we will find precious truths that cannot be ignored. If we are determined to know Him in that manner, He will take the time to show us His glory."

END NOTES

[1] Merriman-Webster.com/dictionary/hearing

[2] Merriman-Webster.com/dictionary/listening

[3] Merriman-Webster.com/dictionary/knowing

[4] Wikipedia.org/transverse myelitis

[5] Merriam-Webster.com/dictionary/presumption

[6] ask.com/wiki/catheter_ablation (an invasive procedure used to remove a faulty electrical pathway from the hearts of those who are prone to developing cardiac arrhythmias such as atrial fibrillation, atrial flutter, supraventricular tachycardia)

[7] Wikipedia.org/wiki/Jim_Jones

[8] Merriman-Webster.com/dictionary/presumption

[9] Merriman-Webster.com/dictionary/paradigm shift

[10] WhatIs.com/6° of separation

[11] Adam Clarke's Commentary, Electronic Database. Copyright © 1996, 2003, 2005, 2006 by Biblesoft, Inc.

[12] Pantages, George, *Unraveling the Mysteries of Faith.* Cedar Park, Texas, 2010

[13] ask.com/wiki/chicken_game

[14] etonline.com/dailyfirst/143214_Biggest_Loser_Scandal

[15] (Interlinear Transliterated Bible. Copyright © 1994, 2003, 2006 by Biblesoft, Inc.

[16] Cline,AustinWilderness: Profile of the Wilderness, Frequently Described in the Bible

[17] Merriman-Webster.com/dictionary/wilderness

[18] http://blog.chron.com/thetexican

George Pantages Ministries

BOOKS AVAILABLE IN ENGLISH

LIBROS DISPONIBLES EN ESPAÑOL

GEORGE PANTAGES
Cell 512-785-6324
GEOPANJR@YAHOO.COM
GEORGEPANTAGES.COM